The Heavenly People
Going underground with Brother Yun and the Chinese House Church

by Eugene Bach and Brother Zhu
Edited by Luther Martin

The Heavenly People
Going underground with Brother Yun and the Chinese House
Church

by Eugene Bach and Brother Zhu
Edited by Luther Martin

Published by
Fifth Estate, Post Office Box 116,
Blountsville, AL 35031

First Edition
Cover Designed by An Quigley

Printed on acid-free paper
Library of Congress Control No: 2011922261
ISBN: 9781936533060

Fifth Estate, 2011

This book is dedicated to
all those who will be the fruit of
the Back to Jerusalem Movement.
It was written for them.

FOREWORD

We were setting up for a *Back to Jerusalem* event in the fall of 2010, in Los Angeles, California. My good friend Brother Yun, also known as the Heavenly Man, would be the main speaker for the evening. I was amazed at the number of people who started to pour in as soon as we opened the doors.

I live in China and help to carry out *Back to Jerusalem* projects in China, the Middle East, South East Asia, and Africa together with Brother Yun. *Back to Jerusalem* is an underground movement that is sending 100,000 missionaries from China to some of the most dangerous places in the world. I am used to living in the shadows, not accustomed to advertising anything on a grand scale. I am certainly not used to setting up large meetings in the West.

Before moving to China, I had served in a special operations group in the US military and had spent some time in intelligence. As it turned out, this was very good preparation for a life of working together with Brother Yun and the underground house churches in China.

We did not have much money to advertise for this event in California, and relied solely on help from our friends and partners in the area. We had just started the *Back to Jerusalem* Facebook page to tell others about the meeting. We started this page in May of 2010 and it was slowly growing in popularity every day. I remember telling the volunteer security personnel from *Karate For Christ International* that I would be happy if only five people, other than our team, came to the event and filled up the first row.

When I walked outside to get a better view of what was going on, one man walked by me with a group following him. I stretched out my hand and greeted him, "Welcome! It is so great to have you with us this evening. Where are you coming from?"

"We drove all the way from Boston, Massachusetts [very far away from California], just arrived, and we aim to get a front seat, so forgive me if I just keep walking."

Never would I have imagined so many people in attendance, after so little public advertisement! I remember thinking, "How did people on the East Coast even know about this meeting?"

I said to Brother Yun, before he knelt down to pray over the evening, "I can't believe how many people are coming to this church tonight. I don't even know how they found out about the meeting." Brother Yun looked at me with a big smile and simply exclaimed, "Hallelujah!" Nothing more needed to be said.

I have known Brother Yun long enough to know and to trust that he will humble himself before God and preach the message of the Gospel, whether there are 10,000 people in an auditorium, a handful of officials in a government office, or just one lost soul in a living room.

Why is Brother Yun called the Heavenly Man? It is our goal to share his amazing, miraculous story with you in these pages. What God did in his life is truly remarkable, but even more powerful is what God is doing today through the Christians in China.

To understand Brother Yun, you must first understand the vision that keeps his heart beating. He believes that God has called him to help introduce and support the vision of the underground house churches of China in what is called the *Back to Jerusalem* vision. You must grasp this vision in order to truly appreciate Brother Yun and the story of his life. The calling that God placed on his heart runs through the very blood in his veins and consumes his every waking moment. To fully comprehend the *Back to Jerusalem* vision, you must first understand the history of the underground house churches in China.

I was in Chiang Mai, Thailand, 8 years earlier, when leaders from several of the main house church networks in China came to reconfirm what they had already affirmed in the year 2000 in Myanmar. I personally witnessed their anointing of Brother Yun to represent the underground house churches and their vision of *Back to Jerusalem* to the outside world.

I did not know it then- maybe they did not even know it- but during that time in Chiang Mai, they were anointing Yun to introduce a vision and a concept that the Western world had no modern understanding of. There was no reference point in the contemporary Western model to what the Chinese church was planning to do.

Although the underground house churches and the *Back to Jerusalem* vision are unique in the world today, their example can be found splashed across the pages of the book of Acts in the Bible. The term "Back to Jerusalem," as it is taught in the underground house churches of China, has been debated, written about, attacked, supported, studied, taught, and dissected in Western theological seminaries, but remains completely unique in the world today.

What is the Back to Jerusalem vision? What is the vision of the underground house churches in China?

Back to Jerusalem is what the Chinese consider to be their part in the "Great Commission." Jesus gave the Great Commission to His disciples in the book of Matthew, commanding them to spread the Good News to every tribe, tongue, and nation. The underground house churches in China believe that Jesus also gave them the *Back to Jerusalem* vision.

There are entire books written about this unique topic, but to keep it simple, "Back to Jerusalem" is the vision given to the Chinese underground house churches to take the Gospel of Jesus Christ into every country, town, city, village and tribal group between China and Jerusalem. This is the last stretch and final frontier for the gospel. The region between China and Jerusalem is the most unevangelized area in the world today and, as can be expected due to the lack of Christians, it is also the most poverty-stricken and lacking in basic human rights. More unreached people groups live in this area than in any other place on earth, but few of the world's Christian resources actually target this area.

Brother Yun travels around the world, sharing about the vision of the Chinese house churches. He and his family have dedicated their lives to this vision that God has clearly given to them, and their task is not small. They work tirelessly to help reshape the way that the world views missionary work. Brother Yun has also been called to missionary-sending countries, to share the message that they are doing some things incorrectly. He has been asked to go and to cast the vision in areas where it is not yet understood.

It often seems that Brother Yun is standing in front of an army of critics who either don't understand the *Back to Jerusalem* vision or, for reasons that can't be explained, don't want to understand it. When hearing of the attacks against him by fellow brothers and sisters in Christ, I often wonder if Brother Yun wouldn't rather be back in a Chinese prison, beaten by unbelievers, than to have to grapple with the heartbreak of fellow Christians openly attacking him in the most vicious of ways.

Why did God choose Brother Yun for this task? How did God prepare him for the job of going out into the world and sharing the vision of the Chinese house churches?

For the answers we must go back in time, to the early days of the house church movement in China.

Eugene Bach

INTRODUCTION

The Chinese church is one of the greatest miracles in modern history. Never before have so many people in so short a time had their lives completely transformed by the power of the Gospel of Jesus Christ. Experts have approximated that every day, thirty thousand Chinese give their lives to Christ in China. Every day, Chinese of all ages and walks of life are coming to realize that lasting joy cannot be found in the wealth and power that their quickly developing nation promises them. China has indeed become a world superpower, but the fast pace of economic development has left many people searching for a joy that cannot be bought. Many are finding out that even the best education and the highest paying jobs cannot provide them with the love, peace, and joy that can only be found in Christ.

There are most likely more than 130 million Christians in China today, with estimates as high as 150 million. These believers are not just people who go to church on Sundays and live their lives like everyone else during the rest of the week. These are committed Christians who have encountered the Living God and are willing to endure much hardship for the sake of the gospel. These are Christians who have been freed from slavery to sin, and are committed to glorifying the God who freed them by taking His message not only throughout China, but even to the ends of the earth. These vast millions understand the darkness and hopelessness from which they came, and desperately desire to pull others out before it is too late.

The millions of souls coming to faith in Jesus throughout China did not come without a price. Hundreds of missionaries from faraway lands poured out their blood on Chinese soil so the seed of the gospel could grow. Then, with the forced expulsion of all missionaries after 1949, the Chinese church was freed from outside influence and has since grown into the mighty army we see today.

This growth came at great cost for the Chinese as well. For decades, Chinese Christians have endured all manner of suffering and deprivation for the sake of their Lord Jesus. Throughout the second half of the 20th century, countless thousands of Chinese believers were brutally beaten, tortured, imprisoned, and even killed for their faith. By the 1970s, it was believed that no Christians remained alive in China, but this was far from the truth.

Jesus said that a grain of wheat must fall into the ground and die before it can bear any fruit (John 12:24). The history of the Chinese church proves this truth. Just when the rest of the world thought there weren't any Christians left in China, a revival started. The same God who had raised His Son from the dead on the third day also resurrected the Chinese church! Small Christian gatherings in homes began to appear all over China and the house church movement was born. The few Bibles still left in China were painstakingly copied by hand and distributed to various places. Streams of living water were going forth in a land that had been dry and thirsty for so long.

Unlike earlier Chinese Christians, who had been heavily divided by competing Western theologies, this new generation was refined in the fires of persecution and had a truly Chinese understanding of the gospel. Having God's Word free from Western thoughts and traditions allowed it to spread unhindered across China. As the fire of the gospel spread throughout the land, many miracles also took place (some of which you will read about in this book). Chinese Christians have now become a testimony to Christians around the world as to what it means to take up one's cross and follow Jesus.

This book is a factual account of the life of one of the countless Chinese who was part of the Chinese church's rebirth in the 1970s. His life is the testimony of an ordinary man from the humblest of circumstances being mightily used by an extraordinary God. In this brother's story you will see the endless love of Christ, the infinite power of the One True God, and the great sacrifice that was needed to bring God's love to the Chinese people. You will also get a glimpse of the wonderful plan God has for the Chinese church—the *Back to Jerusalem Movement*—and how God is using the Chinese to accomplish His will on earth. As you read, it is our prayer that you too will come to meet this Jesus, who died on the cross for your sins over 2000 years ago so that you might have life abundant and eternal.

CHAPTER 1

Just as the Cultural Revolution began to decline, out of the ashes a light started to shine in Henan Province. This light had never been fully extinguished, but had been buried in the hearts of persecuted Christians for decades. At last the time had come for the light to no longer lie hidden under a basket, but to shine forth in one of the darkest times in China's history. In the same way that Jesus was born in a humble stable (not in a princely palace) and spent most of His time among the poor and despised of His day (not at the tables of kings), so also His love spread first in the humble villages of destitute Henan farmers.

In one of these small farming villages, in Nanyang County, there lived a poor family of seven. Like most farmers in that area, they lived in a simple home, made of straw and mud, that was icy cold in the winter and unbearably hot in the summer. Growing enough food to feed such a large family required that everyone work in the field from a young age, meaning that their educational opportunities were severely limited.

The hard-working mother of five had grown up during the turbulent times leading up to the communist revolution and had a secret from her past: unbeknownst to the rest of the family, she had given her life to Jesus as a young lady in the 1940s. Back then, a missionary had come to her town with the gospel and many lives had been changed. However, she had only been able to learn a few hymns and Bible stories before the communists took over in 1949 and scattered the young believers. The new government quickly expelled all missionaries and imprisoned or killed the local pastors. Without Biblical instruction or fellow Christians to learn from, her love for the Lord gradually grew cold and her faith was almost forgotten for decades.

The father of the household was a battle-hardened ex-soldier of the defeated Nationalist army. Among the local community he was known for his violent temper and general hatred of others. He taught his children to work hard and to be cruel toward others. At the same time, he loved his family and did his best to protect them. Over time he developed lung cancer, which later spread to his stomach. The doctor said his situation was hopeless and that the family should prepare for his death. In vain, he sought out a Daoist priest to cast out the "evil spirits" he believed were the cause of the sickness, but his health only grew worse. Though the family was already poor, the father's sickness intensified their poverty, leading the fourth child—known around the world today as Brother Yun—to drop out of school in order to join his brothers and sisters in begging for food from their neighbors.

It was in the midst of this most desperate and seemingly hopeless situation that Yun's mother remembered the faith of her youth. One night while in bed, she heard a gentle voice say, "Jesus loves you." Immediately she recognized the call of her loving Savior and fell on her knees in tearful repentance. That night she gave her life back to Jesus Christ and never turned away from Him again. Though she had turned her back on God for many years, He had never turned His back on her.

Remembering the words she had heard so many years ago, she knew that nothing is impossible for God. She quickly gathered the family together and told them that Jesus was the only hope for their father. When she told them her testimony, they all committed their lives to the Lord and began to pray fervently for his healing. All night they laid hands on him and cried out, "Jesus, heal father!"

To the joy of all, the next morning he had an appetite for the first time in months. His health rapidly improved and within a week he was completely healed of cancer! Where the doctors and superstitions had proved useless, the Creator of the universe had not only proved His existence, but also His power to heal. It was indeed a miraculous work of the Lord. This miracle served as a spark to bring salvation to many.

They immediately wanted to share this great news with everyone they knew, but had to be careful because unauthorized public meetings were illegal at that time. They decided to send the children out to invite friends and family to their home. Since everyone had known about Yun's father's ailing health, many assumed that he must have died. Some even came expecting it to be a funeral. Imagine the shock when a completely healed and healthy man came to the door to invite them in!

After everyone had arrived, the doors were locked and the windows were covered to protect the meeting from prying eyes. Once everything was secure, Yun's parents explained the great miracle that the Lord had done when they simply prayed to Jesus. That night everyone present knelt down on the floor and gave their lives to Jesus Christ.

From that time on, Brother Yun, born Liu Zhenying, had a deep desire to be close to Jesus and to serve the Lord with all his heart. His mother did her best to preach and to lead the new Christians in their home, but her lack of Scriptural knowledge and inability to read was somewhat limiting. Nevertheless, God used her mightily and some of those to whom she ministered later went on to become preachers in the Chinese house churches.

She told Yun that all Jesus' teachings were written down in the Bible, but sadly there weren't any Bibles left. Rather than being discouraged, this only increased Yun's desire to have a Bible and to read Jesus' teachings for himself. He was determined and would not rest until he had a Bible in his hands.

In those days, owning a Bible was a very dangerous thing. If caught by the authorities, the owner's entire family would be severely beaten and the Bible would be burned. Most of the remaining Bibles in China had been buried to prevent discovery, and only a few older Christians could even remember what a Bible looked like. Not only were people all over China left physically starving because of the utter failure of the "Great Leap Forward," but the Cultural Revolution had also created a famine of the Word of God.

When reflecting on those times, Yun recounts, "We didn't have any Bibles. We didn't have any pastors. We didn't have any places of worship…but Jesus' love never left China. People may expel the missionaries and burn the Bibles, but no one can take God's love away from us."

Yun heard about an old man who lived in another village and had been a pastor before the Cultural Revolution. Yun and his mother visited him, hoping to see his Bible. After spending 20 years in prison for his faith, the old man was afraid and wasn't willing to admit to anyone that he had a Bible. All he said was, "The Bible is a heavenly book. Only the God of heaven can provide it for you, so you must pray to God. He is always faithful to those who seek Him."

Yun took those words to heart and began to intensely pray for a Bible. Every night he would kneel down in his room, on a stone he had brought in for this purpose, and simply pray, "Lord, please give me a Bible. Amen." After a month of praying like this, a Bible still hadn't appeared.

He went back to the old pastor and pleaded with him to allow him just to glance at the Bible and maybe copy down a few words from it. The pastor's response was that prayer was not enough, but he would also have to fast and weep in order to receive a Bible.

Yun again heeded the pastor's words and for the next one hundred days ate nothing for breakfast or lunch. At this point, his parents started to think he was going insane. Yun remembers that time as one of the most difficult in his life.

After months of waiting, while praying in the early hours of the morning, Yun received a vision from the Lord. In the vision, he was pushing a heavy cart up a hill on his way to beg for food in a nearby village. Because fasting had weakened him, he had great difficulty pushing the cart and it almost fell back on him. Then he saw a kind-looking old man pulling a large cart of wonderful-smelling fresh bread in the opposite direction, down the hill. There were also two younger men walking beside the cart. With a compassionate look on his face, the old man asked Yun if he was hungry and Yun immediately burst into tears. The old man then took a red bag out of his cart and told the two men to give it to Yun, who opened it to find a fresh bun inside. As he put the bread into his mouth, it suddenly turned into a Bible! The vision ended with Yun kneeling on the ground with his Bible, thanking the Lord and promising to serve Him for the rest of his life.

Yun quickly woke from the vision and started searching all over the house for the Bible. After realizing it had only been a dream, he wept so loudly that he woke up his parents. The more they heard about his vision, the more they were convinced he had lost his mind. All they could do was hold him tightly and weep together before the Lord, asking God to give their son a Bible before he went mad.

They continued in this fashion for some time, until they heard a faint knock at the door. Before unlocking the door, Yun asked, "Are you bringing bread to me?" The voice outside replied in the affirmative, and Yun recognized the voice as the one from his vision. He quickly opened the door and saw the two men from the vision standing there, one with a red bag in his hand. As the mysterious visitors disappeared into the night, Yun opened the bag without delay and was overjoyed to find his very own Bible inside, a miraculous gift from God. The Bible was the first gift Yun received from God in prayer.

Although the time of waiting had been difficult, the Lord used it to teach him the importance of perseverance in prayer—something that would become absolutely vital for surviving the hardships he would face in the future. The experience also gave him an insatiable hunger for God's Word that hasn't left him to this day. So often, we get impatient or even angry with God for not giving us the things we ask for right away, but God has His own timing and only the best reasons for delaying. If God had simply dropped a Bible in Brother Yun's lap the moment he started to pray for it, perhaps he wouldn't have treasured it as much as he did after months of deep longing for the Word. Although we may not understand it, God always has a reason for what He does and His ways are infinitely higher than ours, *"For as the heavens are higher than the earth, so are My ways higher than your ways, and My thoughts than your thoughts."* (Isaiah 55:9)

Yun later found out more about the two men and the events that had led up to him receiving the Bible. An old evangelist, who had also suffered greatly during the Cultural Revolution, had sent the men from a faraway village. He had buried his Bible inside a can, deep in the ground, with the hope that one day he would be able to dig it up and read it again. Around the time that Yun had started his fast, the Lord had shown the old man in a vision the exact location of Yun's house and told him to send the Bible to the young man living there. The old man may have been a little skeptical at first, as it took him a few months before finally deciding to obey the Lord's command. He eventually gave the Bible to the two young men and asked them to deliver it to Yun.

The miraculous way that Yun was given a Bible only strengthened his faith in God's Word. From the very beginning of His walk with the Lord, he never doubted that the Bible is God's eternal and infallible revelation to all mankind.

From that time on, Yun read his Bible from morning until late at night every day. Whenever he had to work on the farm, he would carry the Bible with him into the fields and read it at every opportunity. He loved God's Word so much that he even slept with the Bible on his chest.

He had a slight problem, however; because of the demands of the farm, Yun had only had three years of school education. To make matters worse, the Bible he had been given was written in traditional Chinese characters, whereas schools in China at that time only taught simplified characters. In order to understand the Bible, he had to look up every character in a dictionary, which was a very slow and arduous process. In this manner, he read through the entire Bible, one word at a time.

After reading through the Bible once, he took to memorizing one chapter a day. He began with the Gospel of

Matthew and memorized the entire book in a little less than a month. Then he read through the other three Gospels and started memorizing the book of Acts. It was while memorizing the first chapter of Acts that the Lord led him to meditate on verse 8, *"But you shall receive power when the Holy Spirit has come upon you; and you shall be witnesses to Me in Jerusalem, and in all Judea and Samaria, and to the end of the earth."*

After reading this verse, he realized that he didn't understand who the Holy Spirit is, or how he could receive the power that was promised. His mother didn't know either and simply told him to pray.

In prayer, Yun asked for the power of the Holy Spirit needed to make him into the witness for God he so dearly wanted to become. God responded by giving him overflowing joy and a deep revelation of God's love and presence. From that time on, God would occasionally give Yun new worship songs with which to praise the Lord and to build up the faith of the house churches.

A few days later, after praying and getting into bed, Brother Yun heard the Lord say, "I will send you to the west and to the south to be My witness." He went to his parents' room, thinking his mother had called him, but she said she hadn't and told him to go back to bed. Again the voice spoke to him, and again his mother told him to go back to sleep. Finally, he prayed and said, "If this is You, Jesus, I'm listening. If you're calling me to preach the gospel, I will obey."

Early the next morning, the Lord spoke to Yun in a dream. The same old man from the vision of the bread walked toward him and said, "Face the west and south to preach the gospel and be the Lord's witness there." Next in the dream, he saw a gathering of many people and was told he would be a witness to them. He then laid hands on a demon-possessed woman and cast out the demon in Jesus' name, causing great amazement among the people. A young man then came and asked him to come to his village to preach the gospel. The man said Christians in his village had been fasting and praying for Yun for three days. The man then gave his name, age, and the name of his village.

After sunrise, Yun told his parents he was going out to preach the gospel as the Lord had commanded. Before leaving, he told his mother the name, age, and a detailed description of the young man he saw in the dream, explaining that the man would come to their home that day and that they should keep him there until Yun returned. Having left these instructions, he departed and headed westward, out of the village.

While crossing a bridge, he met an old Christian who said he was just on his way to ask Yun to come and preach in his village in the west. The Christians in the village had been fasting and praying for three days, hoping that the man who had miraculously received a Bible would come and teach it to them. At the early age of 16, Yun's life as a traveling evangelist had begun.

Upon Yun's entry into the village, those working in the fields dropped their tools and ran to him. Between thirty and forty people gathered around him and stared at him intently, absolutely starving to hear God's Word.

At first he didn't know what to do, so he closed his eyes tightly and held his Bible over his head, saying, "God sent me this Bible in answer to my prayers. If you want one, you'll have to pray like I did." They wanted him to teach them, but he had no idea how to, so he recited some of the verses he had memorized and then recited the entire Gospel of Matthew out loud. He spoke quickly, so as not to forget what he had memorized, and then sang some new songs the Lord gave him right at that moment.

God's Word did its work and the crowd was convicted of their sins. All of them knelt before the Lord, repented of their sins, and gave their lives to Jesus. Though Yun was a mere teenager, had never received any Bible training, and was barely literate at the time, the Lord used him powerfully to bring His Word to the poor villagers.

After reciting everything he had memorized, he told them he needed to go to another village to preach and would come back after he had memorized more Scripture. As he was preparing to leave, a young woman in the crowd asked him where he was going. When he said he was going to meet a brother named Yu (the young man in the dream) in order to preach in his village, the woman started to weep and cried, "He is my brother!" God was indeed working to bring His children together.

Another miracle took place on the way back to Yun's hometown. It would normally take about two hours to walk to his village from the village he had just preached in, so he decided to run in order to make sure he didn't keep Yu waiting at his house too long. He ran and recited Bible verses for a few minutes and suddenly found himself entering the town! A trip of a few hours had been shortened to a few minutes. Yun was reminded of a similar event in the eighth chapter of Acts, when the Lord quickly took Philip away to a distant location (Acts 8:39-40).

When he arrived at home, his mother was ecstatic because a man had visited them and was exactly like Yun had described. He had run home to tell the others in his village but later returned to fetch Yun. That night they headed south together, hidden in the darkness, and Yun was able to bless the believers in that village with all of the Bible verses he had memorized.

The fire of the gospel had returned to burn brighter than ever before in China. As Yun faithfully preached to the west and south of his village, churches were planted and over 2,000 people came to Jesus in the first year. It was the beginning of a great revival that would spread not only throughout all of China, but would one day even spill over the border into other lands shrouded in spiritual darkness. The people who walked in darkness had seen a great light!

CHAPTER 2

Brother Yun first met Deling, his wife-to-be, at one of the worship services he led in his home on Sunday nights. She was also one of several new believers he baptized one night in an icy cold river in the dead of winter. Baptisms were usually held late at night, and sometimes it was so cold outside that they would have to cut a hole in the ice in order to baptize people. Hundreds of believers were baptized by Yun in Henan during those days. They assumed the police would rather stay in their warm beds than to go out to arrest Christians. However, on the night that Deling was baptized the authorities did come and arrested over 100 believers. As everyone was lined up for questioning, Yun amazingly managed to slip away into the darkness unnoticed.

Similar to Yun's father, Deling's mother was also miraculously healed of an illness. After her healing and salvation, she was determined for her daughter to marry a preacher (despite protests from everyone else in the family). It ended up that Yun was the only single preacher in the whole area. According to tradition, both of their mothers arranged the marriage together.

As a poor preacher, all Yun could say to his bride before their marriage was, "God has chosen me to be his witness and to follow him through great hardships and the way of the cross. I don't have any money and am always being chased by the authorities. Do you really want to marry me?"

The young and innocent 18-year-old replied, "I will never let you down. I will join with you and we'll serve the Lord together." During all these years, through countless trials and indescribable suffering, she has kept her word and has been the most faithful partner in ministry that a preacher could ever have.

The way of the cross was central in their lives from the very beginning of their marriage. On the day of their intended wedding, Yun and Deling went to the marriage office to apply for their marriage license. Having recognized Yun's name on the registration form, the clerks quickly sent Deling outside and arrested him. This delayed their wedding for some months, but they were finally wed in 1981.

The first few months of their marriage were full of narrow escapes from the law, as they traveled to many areas to illegally preach the gospel. By that time, Yun was on the government's "Wanted List", and posters with his name and picture on them could be seen in all public locations. They weren't even able to return home because the police were waiting for them there. It certainly wasn't an easy way to begin a marriage, but the persecution only brought them closer together and closer to the Lord during that time.

The police also targeted Yun's mother, identifying her as the leader of an unauthorized church meeting. On one occasion, they placed a large dunce cap on her head and paraded her through the village streets. They also forced her to attend communist indoctrination programs called "re-education classes." Despite this constant harassment from the authorities, the gospel quickly spread throughout Henan, which soon became known as the "Galilee of China," after the Judean town where Jesus' disciples came from.

An important event in the history of the Chinese church happened in 1980, when Yun was invited by the government to attend a meeting of religious representatives. The government was forming a "Three Self Patriotic Church" under the authority of the Religious Affairs Bureau. At first, Yun was open to discussing the idea, but other leaders quickly attacked him as a "false Christian" whose activities were disturbing the social order. When he realized that the meeting had deteriorated into Christians being slandered in front of unbelievers, he left with a firm commitment never to mix faith with government affairs again. Rejecting the offer to preach under government control would cost Yun a great deal in the years ahead.

This division between the Three-Self church and the house churches remains to this day, and there are unfortunately many misunderstandings between the two groups. There are doubtless many true and loving Christians in the Three-Self movement, but house church believers cannot understand how the church can remain pure under the authority of an atheistic government. Rather than being restricted by government rules, the house churches prefer to answer only to Jesus Christ, regardless of the cost.

It was from then on that Yun's preaching career in China became one of "fleeing evangelism." He would travel with coworkers to preach the gospel in one location, and then quickly flee to another when the police found out about them. It was not unlike the days of the early church when Jesus told His disciples, *"When they persecute you in this city, flee to another."* (Matthew 10:23)

In this way, God used persecution to spread His message of salvation over many areas and across great distances in a short time. These fleeing evangelists were not allowed to remain in one town for long, so they were always bringing the gospel to new places.

In July 1981, while leading a meeting of 120 believers, Yun was captured and almost sent to prison. By God's grace, the police car taking him to the station got a flat tire, and he was able to escape. The constant running from the police was exhausting and caused Yun to cry out to God for an explanation. If God is all-powerful, why didn't He protect them from persecution?

God's Word provided Yun with the answer he needed: *"To this you were called, because Christ also suffered for us, leaving us an example, that you should follow His steps."* (1 Peter 2:21)

The Lord made it clear to Yun that one reason He allows suffering and persecution is so that we may rely on Him alone. His grace is sufficient for us, so we must submit

ourselves to God and embrace whatever difficulties may come
our way. In life there are seasons of peace and of persecution,
of joy and of grief. All of them are from the Lord and are
designed to conform us into the image of His Son Jesus
(Romans 8:28-29).

During those times of intense persecution in Henan, no
pastor or preacher could return home. The police had raided
their homes, confiscated all their belongings, and set watch in
case they would return. Church meetings were held late at
night to avoid arousing public attention, and the teachers slept
in hiding during the day.

After one late night of preaching in a barn, Yun was
exhausted and went to sleep in a cornfield away from the
meeting place. Eventually the police arrived and broke up the
meeting and arrested those in attendance. They knew Yun was
somehow involved in the meeting and searched desperately for
him in all the buildings. They finally overheard him snoring in
the field and found him. Fortunately, since he had been
sleeping so far away from the meeting place, they couldn't
prove he had anything to do with the gathering and were
forced to let him go.

By 1983, the house churches had grown so numerous
that there was a great need for organization and training of
more evangelists and Bible teachers. There was especially a
great need for teachers among the fledgling churches in other
provinces. After much prayer, the leaders in Henan decided to
send Brother Yun and two young women westward to Shaanxi,
to preach in the churches there.

While praying before they left, Yun saw a frightening
vision. An evil black creature jumped on him and pinned him
to the ground. Its great weight pressed down hard on him and
he could barely breathe. The creature grabbed him by the
throat and started to choke him. With the other hand, it tried to
shut his mouth with a pair of steel pliers. Then Yun saw an
angel come to his aid. He was able to poke the creature in the
eyes so that it fell off of him, and the angel carried him away
while he shouted, "Hallelujah! Jesus' blood has overcome

you!" Yun would come to understand the meaning of the vision in the days that followed.

The three evangelists traveled to Shangnan County in Shaanxi, and three days of meetings were arranged. Yun spoke all day the first day but lost his voice on the afternoon of the second. He asked one of the young women to preach while he went to lie down and rest his voice.

While he lay on the bed and meditated on what he had shared earlier in the day, the door was kicked open and he found himself pinned down by a police officer. Just as in the vision, the officer had his hand on Yun's throat and demanded to know where he came from. Other officers bound Yun tightly with a rope and, seeing a wooden cross on the wall, mockingly took it down and tied it to Yun's back. They then proceeded to kick him fiercely until he was bloodied and bruised.

In this condition, Yun was paraded down the streets with a police car driving in front; announcing on a loudspeaker that he had came from Henan to preach and would be severely punished.

Although the police wanted to make an example of him so as to discourage people from believing in Jesus, they had actually turned Yun into a public testimony of the gospel. When people saw this bloodied man bearing a cross down their streets, many thought "Jesus from Henan" had come, and many people came to know why he was being mistreated and about the message he preached. He had indeed been made a spectacle to the world for the sake of Jesus.

After another severe beating and half a day of parading through the streets, they arrived at the police station and threw him into an interrogation room. As they started to question him, he knew answering them would endanger other Christian coworkers, so he felt led by the Lord to pretend he was insane, just as David in the Bible had done before the Philistine king. He started to roll his eyes around and drool on himself like a madman so that he wouldn't have to speak. Since they knew they couldn't get any information from him, and were beginning to think he was crazy, the officers left the room to make a phone call to Henan so they could find out who he was.

Suddenly Yun was alone in the room, with no one watching him. He felt the Lord say to him, "The God of Peter is your God." Yun quickly remembered the story from the book of Acts in which an angel had opened the prison gates so that Peter could escape. At that moment, the ropes tying his hands behind his back suddenly snapped. Yun held onto the ropes and kept his hands behind his back, in case anyone should return, and opened the door by turning the doorknob with his mouth. Then he walked out of the room and through the courtyard. There were several people in the courtyard, but none of them even seemed to notice Yun. He walked to the area where the toilets were and pulled off the ropes when he was out of sight.

The main gate remained locked, so the only way he could get out was by jumping over a high wall that had sharp glass embedded at the top. His arms were still numb from being tied together for so long, but he knew that leaping over the wall was his only option. He prayed to God for help and pulled himself up as high as he could on the wall. While he dangled from the wall, lacking the strength to pull himself over, a miracle happened. All of a sudden, he felt himself flying through the air, over the wall and even over a large septic tank that was behind it. He landed safely on the other side and ran into the nearby forest. The angel from his dream had helped him to escape, proving once again that nothing is impossible with God.

While wandering through the woods, he ran into a Christian who had been at the meeting he had been teaching at but had left just before the police came. It was God's mercy that he ran into just the right person who could lead him to safety. The man took Yun back to the house where he had been arrested. As the two arrived, the believers in that house were praying loudly for Yun's release. They were truly amazed to see that the Lord had rescued Yun and were greatly encouraged by his testimony. Before sunrise, Yun and the two young women left to preach at another place. Although the authorities searched everywhere for Yun, he arrived safely in Henan a few days later.

At another time, the Lord led Yun and his wife to travel north to preach the gospel. As they prepared to leave, another Christian brother told them of what the Lord had shown him in prayer. He said, "When you and your wife go north, you will encounter danger. But no matter what happens, the Lord will be with you."

The next day, they passed through many bus stations as they traveled toward the north; each displaying "Wanted" posters with Yun's picture. Rather than being afraid, however, Yun and Deling found their refuge in God and had great joy inside. They considered it a great honor to be slandered and humiliated for the sake of Jesus.

The meetings held in the north were powerful and the churches spent many hours praying for their nation and dedicating themselves to the Lord. Contrary to what is often said about the house churches, their members truly love their country and have shed countless tears while praying over their dear homeland and its leaders.

After one meeting, a local brother warned Yun about what the Holy Spirit had shown him, "Within three days some of you will be bound and beaten for the Lord. Some will even lay down their lives for Him." However, the next three days of meetings went on without any problems.

At midnight on the third day, December 17, 1983, the last meeting ended. Following the pattern set by Christ, the hosts washed everyone's feet and Yun washed the feet of his coworkers with many tears. Before leaving, Brother Zhang gave Yun his warm winter scarf, which would later be of great help to Yun.

As everyone was departing to sleep in different homes, a group of men with flashlights stopped them at the outskirts of the village. Some of the believers immediately ran away, but before Yun could escape he was shocked with hundreds of volts of electricity from an electric baton, throwing him into the snow and causing excruciating pain.

As the men rained down blows upon him and four other brothers, Yun heard a gentle voice say to him, "I know." It comforted him greatly to know that the Lord not only knew what he was enduring, but also everything that he was about to endure.

As the men continued to beat him and to demand that he tell them where his coworkers were, he once again feigned insanity and shouted loudly, "I am a heavenly man! I live in gospel village!" They demanded he take them to his coworkers, so he walked down the street in front of them shouting, "I've been arrested by the police! I don't know where the meetings took place because I'm a heavenly man! I'm not from this earth!" In this way he warned all the local Christians of what had happened and gave them a chance to escape.

This event was how Brother Yun became known as "the heavenly man" throughout the house churches in China. The name was first given to him by those who heard him shouting in the street that night and the nickname has stuck ever since.

Once they realized he wasn't going to give them the information they wanted, the police threw Yun and the four other brothers into the back of a tractor and took them to Wuyang City. The five brothers stood tied together on the back of the tractor, singing about the glory of the cross all the way to the police station. There they were thrown into an unheated cell and left to freeze without any coats. In order to keep from freezing, they stayed up all night praying and singing worship songs while Yun banged on an old drum that had been left in the cell. That night they learned that regardless of their situation, wherever the Lord is there is true freedom.

They were sent to prison the next day. As they entered the prison yard, Yun tried to exhort and encourage any other Christians that may have been in the prison by shouting, "A heavenly man has been sent to prison! I'm not like Judas! I will not betray the Lord!"

Later he found out that there were dozens of Christians in that prison, all of whom endured terrible beatings and torture. Not only would the guards beat prisoners, but also, often the worst beatings came from fellow inmates who were offered better treatment for doing so.

On Yun's first morning in prison, the guards practiced martial arts on his body, kicking, punching, and stomping on him until blood gushed from his mouth. It was a difficult time, but during those first few days in prison, Yun was greatly encouraged by one of the brothers who had been arrested with him. Brother Zhen cared for him after his beatings and encouraged him with words from Scripture. Even after Brother Zhen was sent to his hometown for sentencing, his witness had an effect on the other prisoners, many of whom gave their lives to Jesus and started to treat Yun better.

For more than five weeks, Yun endured many brutal interrogations until they finally found out who he was. Although he never told them anything, the prison brought representatives from counties all over Henan to try to identify him.

Finally, on January 25, 1984, officers from Yun's hometown came and recognized him immediately. They were especially cruel to him because he had embarrassed them by eluding capture so many times in the past. As they handcuffed him to a rail in the back of a van and headed back to Nanyang, he knew he was in for a new level of suffering.

On the long drive across bumpy country roads, the handcuffs cut into Yun's wrists so deeply that blood splattered all over the sides of the van. Eventually his wrist bones were even exposed. When the pain was too much to bear, Yun cried out to God for help. The guards heard him praying and responded by shocking him with the electric batons. The pain was so great that Yun thought he was going to explode. He cried again for the Lord to have mercy on him, and the Lord replied, "You suffer so you can share in the fellowship of my suffering." Then came the comforting words, *"Be still, and know that I am God; I will be exalted among the nations, I will be exalted in the earth!"* (Psalm 46:10)

God used those experiences to show Brother Yun how feeble and helpless he was. Yun had started to become proud because of the great successes he had seen in ministry, and he had started to think he was important to God's work. The trials he was enduring brought home to Yun the fact that people are nothing apart from God, and it is only by God's grace that He uses poor sinners to accomplish His work.

As the van brought Yun into his hometown with much pomp and fanfare, he saw signs posted all over the town that called him a "counter-revolutionary" and "reactionary." Many people ran out into the streets to try and catch a glimpse of him. Though he had no idea what new tortures and trials awaited him, he wasn't afraid. God had reminded him of His words in the book of Revelation, *"Do not fear any of those things which you are about to suffer... Be faithful until death, and I will give you the crown of life."* (2:10)

CHAPTER 3

The next part of Yun's testimony contains one of the most incredible miracles of his life. Unfortunately, many have indeed found it to be so inconceivable that they doubt its veracity. Disbelief at this part of Yun's life has actually been the one of the main causes of personal attacks against Brother Yun in recent years.

The attacks continue to this day, despite the numerous eyewitnesses who were with him in prison and can confirm all that happened. As you read on, you must first ask yourself, "What kind of God is my God? Can He really do these kinds of impossible miracles?" The God that Brother Yun serves is the Creator of heaven and earth who can surely do anything!

Yun finally arrived at Nanyang Prison. He was a bloody mess with black eyes, a swollen face, and deep gashes cut in his wrists by handcuffs. Upon arrival, he was brought to yet another interrogation room where the guards mocked him and told him he was a failure. As they repeatedly mocked him and claimed that the church would never triumph against the Communist party, anger and discouragement began to build up in Yun's heart. Then the Lord brought these words to his mind, "The gospel grows through suffering and will spread throughout the world… Truth is always truth and it will always be victorious. Nothing can change that."

The officers continued to threaten him with what they would do to him if he didn't confess his "crimes," but these words comforted him and gave him strength: *"The LORD is my light and my salvation; whom shall I fear? The LORD is the strength of my life; of whom shall I be afraid?"* (Psalm 27:1)

He reasoned with the interrogators, and they agreed to give him some time to regain his strength and to reflect on his past, expecting him to give a full confession when he was ready.

Yun knew that he was about to face a trial unlike any he had experienced before, but that only helped him to cling to God as his refuge. As he pondered on what lay ahead, the Bible's words about persecution and suffering became even more real to him. He was only one of countless saints throughout history who had endured fiery trials for their faith. He was comforted by the same words of truth that had given strength to many suffering Christians over the centuries: *"My brethren, count it all joy when you fall into various trials, knowing that the testing of your faith produces patience."* (James 1:2-3)

"All who desire to live godly in Christ Jesus will suffer persecution." (2 Timothy 3:12)

"Do not fear those who kill the body but cannot kill the soul. But rather fear Him who is able to destroy both soul and body in hell." (Matthew 10:28)

He knew that a severe test was coming, and he was led by the Holy Spirit to fast like Jesus when Satan tempted Him in the wilderness. From that point on, Yun dedicated himself to prayer, fasting, and meditation on God's Word as he awaited further interrogation. On January 25, 1984, he stopped taking food and water altogether.

The prisoners were always on the verge of starvation, so Yun unintentionally won the favor of many of them when he refused to eat his meals and let everyone else share them instead. This opened the door for him to sing gospel songs to them and tell them about Jesus. Most of the prisoners believed their lives were being controlled by fate, but Yun taught them that God rules all things and will one day judge all men who don't repent and receive Jesus as their Savior.

The judge continued to show leniency toward Yun and allowed him to delay interrogation again, giving him more time to meditate on God's Word and to seek God's wisdom on how to answer his accusers. He decided not only to continue fasting, but also to not say a single word to anyone until he was able to see his family.

Weeks passed, during which Yun did not eat or drink at all. It is a scientific fact that human beings cannot live without water for more than a few days, but God was working another miracle in Yun's life.

Although the fast had been dreadfully difficult in the beginning, as Yun's heart began to fully focus on Jesus, he didn't even think about being hungry. The fact that he was able to fast at all under such harsh conditions proved that it was of the Lord. If the fast had been his own idea, he surely would have failed in the first few days, but since it was purely out of obedience to the Lord and a desire to please Him, God strengthened him.

The fast also proved very useful in delaying his interrogation. When carried to the interrogation room, Yun was too weak to move or even speak, so all the guards could do was send him back to his cell.

On the 38th day of the fast, Yun was tempted by Satan. Satan accused him of trying to be more righteous than Jesus by fasting longer than He had. Yun was so exhausted and discouraged that he even contemplated suicide at that point. As his weakened mind and body struggled with this temptation, the Lord reminded him of Revelation 3:8: *"I know your works. See, I have set before you an open door, and no one can shut it; for you have a little strength, have kept My word, and have not denied My name."*

What a comfort it was to know that Jesus knew his works and had prepared a way for him that couldn't be stopped by even the full force of the Chinese government!

During that time, the Lord also gave him a powerful vision in which he saw several iron gates open, one after the other. Then he saw a great crowd of people from various nations worshipping together before the Lord. Yun cried out to God and expressed his frustration that he was then even too weak to preach the gospel, even if the Lord freed him from prison. Then the Lord revealed to him two more Scriptures, *"For the gifts and the calling of God are irrevocable"* (Romans 11:29), and *"Most assuredly, I say to you, he who believes in Me, the works that I do he will do also; and greater works than these he will do, because I go to My Father."* (John 14:12) In this way, the Lord gave him the strength to keep on living.

By this time, rumors started to spread around the town of a man miraculously surviving without food or water for many days inside the prison. Deling immediately knew it must be her husband and prayed all the more for his strength and protection.

The government placed a false prisoner named Li inside Yun's cell to spy on him and to report anything suspicious to the guards. After some time of observing Yun's way of life and God's amazing power in sustaining him during the fast, Li realized that Yun wasn't a criminal at all, but merely a poor Christian pastor. Because of Yun's week condition, Li had to carry him back and forth to the interrogations. One day, while carrying Yun back to the cell, Li confessed his newfound faith in Christ. The one sent to be an informant ended up becoming a dear brother who prayed for Yun while being forced to bring him to the interrogation room.

On one occasion, Yun was taken to the medical clinic for an especially painful type of torture. The guards held Yun's hand and feet down while the doctor jabbed a large needle under his fingernails, one at a time. This pain was too much to bear and Yun eventually lost consciousness.

Many might ask themselves, "How could anyone endure such relentless torture, over and over again?" Yun would tell them that, along with the Scriptures he had memorized, God strengthened him to endure by reminding him of what Jesus suffered on the cross.

No suffering can compare to what Jesus endured for us. He was brutally beaten numerous times, whipped with flesh-tearing lashes, forced to carry His own cross to the execution place, was nailed to the cross, and then forced to die a slow and excruciating death while hanging in the sun for hours.

Not only that, but He received the full measure of God's wrath for our sins, a kind of suffering that is completely inconceivable to us. If anyone can understand Yun's pain, or the suffering of any of us, it is most certainly Jesus.

It gave Yun much encouragement to know that, *"we do not have a High Priest who cannot sympathize with our weaknesses, but was in all points tempted as we are, yet without sin."* (Hebrews 4:15)

Looking back on such despicable torture, Yun can only express thanks to God for preserving him through it. He understood that God had a purpose for allowing him to suffer; namely, to break down the stubbornness and self-centeredness buried deep within Yun's heart. It was through these trials that he learned patience, perseverance, and a deeper love for the family of God.

The interrogations continued for weeks, but Yun still refused to talk. The guards decided to persuade other prisoners to help torment him. They told Yun's cellmates that he was an evil criminal who opposed the government and deserved no pity. They even promised to reduce the sentences of those who were particularly cruel to Yun.

From then on, the cellmates would often urinate on Yun's face and one time even threw him into the septic tank that contained all the prisoners' waste. On that occasion, the guards continually shocked him with electric batons and kicked him, forcing him to roll in the human excrement. If anyone tried to help him, they were electrocuted as well.

Throughout that long winter, the scarf Brother Zhang had given him on the night of his arrest was all he had to keep him warm. All his other clothes had been reduced to rags. That scarf reminded him of the love of the other believers, and he felt as if they were always with him. When the other prisoners maliciously threw it into the toilet, he was tempted to curse them, but then the Lord brought to his memory the command, *"Repay no one evil for evil...Do not be overcome by evil, but overcome evil with good."* (Romans 12:17, 21)

After Yun endured the wrath of the other prisoners, God judged them with a terrible skin disease. Every prisoner except Yun and Li was afflicted. At that point, the guards transferred Li out of Yun's cell because they realized he had been protecting him.

When the prisoners urinated on Yun's face again, they woke up the next morning covered in grotesque pus-filled welts. Again Yun was spared. Then another prisoner named Yu began to show kindness toward Yun. In due time, he also gave his life to Christ and became a replacement for Li. The disease continued to rage among the prisoners, and the leader of the cell tried everything he could to infect Yun; but God protected him, much to the chagrin of the guards and prisoners.

In April of that year, the Lord revealed to Yun's wife and mother that he would survive and that they would be able to see him soon. The only church leader in the area who was not in prison at the time came to them after much prayer and said, "It's time to visit Yun in prison." What God had told them was confirmed when Deling received an invitation from the prison the very next day.

On April 7, Yun's wife, mother, and six other relatives and friends went to the prison. Before allowing him to see his family, the guards whipped and shocked him in the interrogation room until he passed out from the pain. He woke up in the arms of his weeping mother. His body had shriveled so much from the fasting and torture that he was unrecognizable, and his ears had shrunk down to the size of prunes. It wasn't until his mother found his birthmark that they were sure it was he. The shock was too great for Deling, who was over six months pregnant, and she almost fainted.

At that moment, the Lord strengthened Yun and told him it was time to speak. His first words in months were from the Bible, *"Do not put your trust in princes, nor in a son of man, in whom there is no help."* (Psalm 146:3) *"It is better to trust in the LORD than to put confidence in princes."* (Psalm 118:9)

He then encouraged them to be strong in the Lord Jesus Christ, exhorting them to preach the gospel, for the harvest was ripe. He explained to them how that morning the Lord had showed him that he would meet with them. Amazingly, the guards didn't seem to understand what they were saying throughout the whole time they were together, but merely stood there with confused looks on their faces.

Before they parted, one of the friends quickly fetched some crackers and grape juice from a nearby shop so that they could have Communion together. Yun led them in the Lord's Supper, and everyone wept loudly. It was the first food and drink he had taken in 74 days. By a wonderful work of God, Yun had gone without food and water from January 25 to April 7, 1984.

CHAPTER 4

Upon returning to his cell, the guards were utterly incensed that he had eaten and spoken after such a long time. Some of the prisoners were also angry, particularly a Muslim man who told him he deserved to die for believing in Jesus.

After months of silently enduring abuse from guards and prisoners alike, the Holy Spirit moved Yun to speak. The man who had been a mere pile of skin and bones on the floor, and was expected to die in a few days, stood up in front of them all and proclaimed, "Fellow prisoners, I have a message from my Lord. Please listen carefully!"

"God sent me here for your sake. You knew that I was a follower of Jesus from the moment I entered this cell. You have watched me and seen how I haven't taken a single grain of rice or even a drop of water over the last 74 days. In all of history, have you ever heard of anyone who fasted for this long? Can't you see that this miracle is a demonstration of God's mighty power and protection over me?"

"God has enabled me to stand before you today to tell you that Jesus is the true and living God! As you continue in your sin, how do you expect to escape hell on the Day of Judgment?"

"Today the Lord in His abundant mercy is offering you a chance to repent and to receive forgiveness for your sins. You all need to kneel down before Jesus Christ, to confess your sins, and to ask God for forgiveness. How else will you escape the punishment of hell?"

There was dead silence in the cell at first, then the same cell leader who had done so many terrible things to Yun knelt before him and cried out, "Yun, what must I do to be saved?"

Everyone in the cell followed suit and cried out for forgiveness, even the Muslim who had cursed him only moments before. That day, salvation came to cell number two.

The hearts of a roomful of hardened criminals were broken by the power of the gospel. Yun used the few drops of water that they had at the time to baptize every one of them.

From then on, Yun's prison cell became an entirely different place; it became a church of the Living God. Even the guards noticed the drastic change in the prisoners' attitudes, but couldn't understand what had happened. When the cellmates had a chance to go into the yard, they preached the gospel to the prisoners from other cells. Repentance and forgiveness swept through the prison and many were saved. Now Yun's purpose in prison became clear: he had many new believers to disciple.

***

While all these things were happening, Yun's family was enduring many hardships outside the prison walls. Unbeknownst to Yun, Deling was pregnant with their first child. Because it looked like Yun was going to be in prison indefinitely, the local authorities were pressuring her to have an abortion. When she was seven months pregnant, shortly after the prison visit, the government agency for family planning told her, in short, "This child shouldn't be born."

They also told her that she needed to come to the medical clinic in two days to have an abortion. If she didn't come, they would come looking for her to bring her in by force.

Deling was terrified and prayed, "Lord, if this child comes into the world under Your protection, I will entrust him to You." God heard her prayer. The day before she was scheduled to have an abortion, she gave birth to a healthy baby boy, two months early. Moreover, the Lord enabled her to give birth without even the slightest pain.

The day before their son's birth, Yun had a dream from the Lord. In it he saw his wife holding a baby boy. She gently asked him, "What should we name our child?" Immediately a name came to mind and he replied, "His name shall be Isaac." She smiled and took the baby away. Then he woke up.

The following morning, April 19, 1984, a guard came to his cell and said, "Your wife has given birth to a baby boy. She wants you to name him. Here is a pen and paper."

Yun wrote the name he had received in the dream and then took the opportunity to write a note to his son. In it he wrote, "My son, I don't know if I'll ever see you. People want their children to be successful, but your father only wishes that you follow the Lord Jesus and love Him. Isaac, trust and obey the Lord at all times, then you will grow into a man of God. My son, I will see you in heaven. Your father."

Isaac—today a grown man who loves the Lord dearly and has followed in his father's footsteps to become a pastor— gave the following testimony about his birth:

"God is my Father because He gave me life and protected me. Lord, I thank You because You made me in an amazing and excellent way. Your eyes saw me when I was not yet formed in the womb."

For the first few years of his life, the Lord was the only Father Isaac knew.

***

During those days, Christians all over China were being harshly persecuted, but revival continued to sweep through the countryside. Prayer meetings would often last all night, while God healed the sick and many a demon was cast out in Jesus' name. In the midst of the fiery trial brought on by the atheist government, the Word of the Lord went forth and bore fruit throughout the land, as it continues to do to this day.

In a small village roughly 10km from Yun's hometown, there lived a Christian woman with a wealthy husband who worshipped idols. Their son had a terminal illness and they were desperate. Eventually this man allowed local believers to come to their home and prayer for their son. That same night, the Christians had received news of Brother Yun's dire situation in prison and were greatly distressed. As they cried out in prayer for him, they completely forgot about the boy they had originally come to pray for.

The man, who had many high connections in the government, complained to them all, saying, "Stop crying for this Yun! Please pray for my son. If this Jesus whom Yun trusts helps my son, then I'll use my connections to help him get out of prison."

The believers complied and prayed for the boy. He was miraculously healed that very night! The whole family received Jesus, and the joyful father saw to it that the whole village heard the gospel.

It turned out that this man had a cousin who was a guard at Yun's prison. When he heard of all that had happened, this guard felt guilty for mistreating Yun and did what he could to improve Yun's situation. From then on, the persecution abated and Yun was even promoted to be cell leader.

Yun's new position allowed him to better care for all the new disciples, but it also included some unexpected responsibilities. In cell nine was a murderer awaiting execution, who was soon placed under Yun's care. This madman had tried to kill himself numerous times and had also injured others. He was so dangerous that his arms and legs had to be tightly bound at all times. Even then, he would try to bite off the ear or nose of anyone who came too close to him. Yun was given the task of making sure the inmate didn't harm himself or others before his execution, also being warned that he would be held personally responsible if anything went wrong.

When Yun told his cellmates about their expected guest, they all protested and were terrified of having such a "devil" in their cell. Yun reminded them that they had all been like this man before they believed in Jesus. He said they needed to have mercy on the man and to treat him as if he was

Jesus Himself. The cellmates immediately changed their attitudes and began to eagerly await his arrival.

The next morning, this wild man was brought into their cell. His mouth spewed forth hatred and filthy language, and he tried every way he could to cut himself with the chains that bound him. This mass of venomous rage had once been a promising young man named Huang. He was just 22 years old.

After being beaten like an animal and denied food for days by the inmates in his previous cell, Huang had no reason to think things would be better with his new cellmates. What a shock it must have been when he entered Yun's cell and was immediately greeted with love and compassion.

God enabled the prisoners to love Huang like a brother. They all donated some of their precious drinking water to wash him and clean his wounds. Yun tore off part of his own blanket to use for his bandages. Huang just stared at them as they kept on blessing him throughout the day and spent time in worship together. At lunchtime they all shared their rice with him. Yun had to feed him because of his chains. Then there was dinner in the evening.

The best food the prisoners ever received was a steamed bun called a *mantou*. They usually only received one of these buns each week, so the inmates coveted them dearly. That night they received their weekly *mantou*, and Yun decided it was all right for everyone to eat theirs without sharing that night.

As he bit into his *mantou*, a dark cloud came over Yun's heart. The Lord was convicting him of not sharing his *mantou* with Huang. He felt Jesus saying to him, "I died for you on the cross. How can you show your love for me? When I am hungry, thirsty, and in prison, if you do these things to the least of my brothers, you do them to me."

Yun knew what God wanted him to do, but he was so hungry that he resisted. Then the Scripture came to mind, *"Who shall separate us from the love of Christ? Shall tribulation, or distress, or persecution, or famine, or nakedness, or peril, or sword?"* (Romans 8:35) As soon as he wrapped the *mantou* in a cloth and decided to give it to Huang later, he felt the dark cloud lift and his heart was filled with peace and joy.

After breakfast the next morning, Huang started complaining loudly to the guard because he was still hungry. Yun knew exactly what to do. He quickly stood with his back toward Huang, broke the bread behind his back, and dropped the pieces into Huang's bowl.

This was the act that finally broke Huang's heart. He fell over on the floor and wept, saying, "My own parents, my brother and sister, and my fiancé have all disowned me. Why do you love me like this? I can't do anything for you now, but after I'm dead I'll come back as a ghost and serve you for this kindness."

Yun replied, "We treat you this way because Jesus loves you. If we didn't know Jesus, we would treat you just as terribly as the men in your last cell. You need to thank God for His Son, Jesus Christ."

Hearing this, the suicidal murderer tearfully received the love of Christ and was set free from his burden of sin. Just as the thief who was crucified on the cross next to Jesus received forgiveness in his final moments, so Huang was forgiven and would soon be with Jesus in paradise.

Huang had lived a reckless life of crime. When he was only twenty he joined a gang, which cost him his fiancé and put him in jail. His influential father was able to secure his early release, but the young man couldn't find any satisfaction in life.

When he killed his friend in a failed suicide pact, Huang decided he was going to run from the law and travel all over the country experiencing all the sinful pleasures he could, before saying goodbye to his family and killing himself. He used a knife to rob stores and to rape women wherever he went. He tried to find peace for his soul in Buddhist temples, but his condition only got worse.

When he returned to his hometown, to say his last goodbyes to his family, the police finally caught him in some bushes. On his person they found his knife and a suicide note he had written that contained a full confession of his crimes. There was no way he could escape the full force of the law this time.

The same Huang who had committed all these terrible crimes could now be heard praising his Lord and Savior at the top of his lungs inside his prison cell. Actually, it wasn't the same man but a new creation in Christ. He had been completely transformed by the love of Jesus.

Yun and the others etched a large cross and Bible verses into the walls of their cell, which gave Huang great joy in his final days. Those etchings remained on the walls for some time and served as a testimony to the hundreds of prisoners who would later pass through that cell.

Yun baptized Brother Huang on August 16th. The next day, Huang wrote a letter to his parents telling them about his newfound faith and urging them to believe in Jesus. Yun promised to visit them if he was ever released.

At 8 a.m. on August 18th, Huang was called out of his cell for the last time. As he was being taken to the execution ground, his last words were, "I'll see you in heaven!"

Moments later, a shot rang out. Brother Huang had been received into the arms of Jesus.

***

Yun kept his promise to Brother Huang and visited his family shortly after he was released from prison, three-and-a-half years after Huang's execution.

He shared with them their son's final request: that they believe in Jesus. Due to their high positions as Communist Party members, they were quite resistant at first and tried to send Yun away with some money.

Yun could see that the Holy Spirit was working in them, so he refused the money and very boldly told them to receive Jesus as their Savior. At last they dropped to their knees and gave their lives to the Lord. They have been faithful Christians ever since.

CHAPTER 5

On the morning of Brother Huang's execution, Yun was finally taken for his court hearing. He had been tortured in prison for months without being sentenced. In China, a court hearing is more of an assignment of punishment than anything else. The defendant is already assumed to be guilty and the trial is just a formal attempt to extract a confession before issuing a verdict. In Yun's case, the local judges had not been able to get him to say anything incriminating at all, so he was sent to a higher court.

Yun was brought before the Prefecture People's Court. Things did not seem to bode well for him at first. Without thinking, he infuriated the head judge by accidentally sitting down in his chair. Yun's trial was held in a large courtroom with many judges and officials present.

The evidence was presented against him: his Bible, some of his devotional books and notebooks, and secretly recorded tapes of his sermons. When asked to examine the evidence, he was greatly encouraged by the opportunity to handle his old ministry tools. He admitted that they were his, and then the judged pressed him to divulge information about his coworkers. He said he didn't know anything about them.

The court took a 30-minute recess and came back with Yun's sentence: four years of hard labor. Four years…what a far cry this was from the threats of execution that had loomed over his head during the past several months! He was taken to Xinyang Prison Labor Camp a few days later. It was October 1984.

There were over 5,000 prisoners in the labor camp, divided into four work units. Yun's unit had over 1,000 inmates. Everyone had to work fourteen hours a day, seven days a week, at some of the most backbreaking tasks imaginable. Yun was assigned to dig fishponds by hand. He had to climb up and down ladders all day with heavy loads of dirt on his back. Everyone was watched carefully and beaten severely with rifle butts if they appeared to be slacking off.

The inadequate amount of food, combined with the intense labor, caused Yun to collapse many times. At the end of a day's work, he was often too exhausted to crawl into his bunk and simply lay on the floor until morning.

God granted him favor with others in the camp. The injustices he had suffered were so obvious that even the camp warden thought Yun didn't deserve to be there. Over time, resentment built up in Yun's heart and he started to feel sorry for himself. Self-pity would have gotten the better of him had God not reminded him, "This is my will for you. You should walk in it."

The warden, once he saw that he could trust Yun, eventually gave him the easier job of fertilizing the vegetable garden with human excrement. He was also assigned to wash clothes and to help illiterate prisoners to write home to their families. The latter proved to be an effective door for evangelism.

His family was able to visit him on occasion. They hid portions of Scripture in the food and in other gifts they brought. One time Deling even hid parts of the Bible inside a loaf of bread!

Another time, two brothers from the house churches came to check on him and to give him an update on what was happening in the outside world. In a breach of camp regulations, the warden allowed Yun's friends to come inside the prison yard. They were able to have some privacy in the toilet block and shed many tears together in prayer on the dirty floor. The brothers informed Yun about the revival that was continuing to spread around the country. Thousands and thousands were coming to Christ every day. To this day, many Christians in China consider 1985 to be a year of spiritual breakthrough in their country.

While they knelt in fervent prayer, Yong, a prisoner notorious for reporting on other inmates, came into the toilet block and saw them. As Yong started to shout out threats, Yun was filled with the Holy Spirit and commanded him, "In the name of Jesus, how dare you speak against the Living God? Kneel down right now and repent of your sins. Receive the Lord and perhaps He will forgive you!"

At that instant, Yong fell to his knees and gave his life to Jesus. One of the most hated prisoners in the camp became Yun's brother in the Lord. The event reminded Yun that God can perform miracles under all circumstances. Though we may be caught by surprise, God never is!

Yong developed a deep passion for God's Word. One day the guards caught him reading Yun's Bible and took it away from him. At that time Captain Wong, who had been friendly to Yun in the past, was at the prison gate. Yun went to him and politely asked to have his Bible back. Instead, he took the Bible with him back to his office.

Several days later, Yun was called to Captain Wong's office. The captain, suffering from a chronic throat infection, quietly confided in Yun that he had been reading the Bible, but couldn't understand it. The Lord was working in Captain Wong's heart.

Yun seized the opportunity and said, "In order to understand the Bible, you must first accept Jesus into your heart. Trust him and he will help you understand everything in the book. This Bible will not only show you the way to salvation, but Jesus can also heal your throat infection."

Right then and there Captain Wong repented of his sins, professed faith in Jesus, and asked God to heal him. Soon he was completely healed.

God also blessed the Captain with a promotion, allowing him to help Yun more. Yun was transferred to the blacksmith's shop, which gave him more privacy for discipleship and time to study the Bible. He was also given the job of feeding the fish in the ponds and of tending the sheep. This gave him many opportunities to share the gospel with prisoners working at the ponds. He learned a valuable lesson from tending the sheep: You must feed sheep, not beat them, if you want them to follow you. This lesson reinforced his lifelong commitment to feeding the churches God's pure and satisfying Word.

As more and more prisoners believed the gospel, Yun became constantly busy discipling new Christians. Year after year went by, and the end of his sentence was rapidly approaching.

Around three months before his scheduled release, Yun and his cellmates were suddenly woken up in the middle of the night and questioned by officers from the central government. Yun was tied to a flagpole in the center of the prison yard and accused of committing new crimes against the government.

The police had confiscated various materials at his home that he had received from overseas Chinese. Among them was a letter from Brother Xu, the most wanted pastor in China at the time. This alarmed the police because the letter was about planning an attempt to meet with the American evangelist Billy Graham during his upcoming trip to China— an event that was supposed to be secret.

They also had some very incriminating evidence against Yun personally. His reply to Brother Xu's letter had been smuggled out of prison, only to be intercepted by the authorities. In the letter he had described the miserable situation inside the prison camp and pointed out that he had been arrested because of his love for God and his passion for lost souls. The government was not pleased at all.

Yun was moved to another location and locked in solitary confinement. The tiny cell was only about a meter tall and less than a meter wide, making it impossible for him to stand up or fully lie down. There was only one small window on the iron door from which a little light came in.

A day later, an officer told Yun all the new accusations that were being brought against him and sent him to the torture room. There he was shocked with electric batons and beaten with sticks and whips, to the point that his flesh was ripped open all over his body. Before he passed out from the pain, the Lord spoke to his heart, "This is your calling. Patiently endure for the Word of God and the testimony of Jesus."

The worst part about the whole situation wasn't the tiny frigid cell or the torture, but the fact that he didn't have a Bible. He cried out to the Lord for a Bible, and, amazingly, the prison director gave him one. No Bibles or Christian literature of any kind were ever permitted in prison, so this was nothing short of a miracle. Through this incident, the Lord reminded Yun that He had not forgotten him and that He was in complete control of Yun's life. As Jesus said, *"Are not five sparrows sold for two copper coins? And not one of them is forgotten before God. But the very hairs of your head are all numbered. Do not fear therefore; you are of more value than many sparrows."* (Luke 12:6-7)

Yun remained in solitary confinement for three months. By the small amount of light that came in through the little window of his cell, he was able to read through the entire Bible and to memorize 55 chapters.

During that time of being completely cut off from human interaction, he had deep and intimate fellowship with the Lord. God gave him insight into the future of the Chinese house churches and revealed to him how they would take the gospel to the tribes and nations that had never heard the name of Jesus. It was behind those prison bars and iron doors that Yun's heart was set aflame for the *Back to Jerusalem* vision.

As the weeks passed, he did not know what was going to happen to him. He was all but sure that they would execute him this time, yet his heart was at peace. *"You will keep him in perfect peace, whose mind is stayed on You, because he trusts in You."* (Isaiah 26:3)

One morning, he was taken out of his cell and put before a judge and several officials. They told him that his situation was serious and that he could face the death penalty if he didn't cooperate and tell them about his coworkers.

Without even a hint of fear, Yun stood up and raised his bound hands to heaven. He told them, "I am fully prepared to die! I will not answer you. Do whatever you want to me!"

They assured him that the death penalty was not their intention, asked some questions, and sent him back to his cell to think about how he should answer them. He never saw those men again.

Much to his surprise, a few days later he was taken out of his tiny cell and sent to his hometown for yet another trial. Upon arrival in Nanyang, he was taken to a meeting of local Communist Party representatives, government officials, and some leaders of the Three-Self Church.

The police chief said to him, "According to the law, we should give you a longer sentence, but we think you are too stubborn to change your ways. We've decided to let you go home."

Then he warned, "No matter how clever you think you are, if you continue to stir up your followers against our nation's religious policy, you will suffer the consequences for the rest of your life."

With this threat ringing in his ears, Yun was put on a bus going to his home village. It was exactly four years to the day since he had been brought to Nanyang as a bloody mess in the back of a police van. Yun was free!

CHAPTER 6

Reflecting on his first time in prison, Brother Yun has said, "I suffered horrible torture; was dragged in front of judges and courts; was hungry, thirsty, and even fainted from exhaustion, but God was faithful."

"Through it all, God was always faithful and loving to me. He never left me nor forsook me. His grace was always sufficient and He provided for my every need."

Yun believes that it isn't those imprisoned and tortured for the sake of the gospel that truly suffer, but those who never experience God's presence in their lives. What kept Yun alive and joyful in the midst of such deplorable conditions was the joy and peace that he experienced daily in fellowship with Jesus Christ.

Jesus said, *"Peace I leave with you, My peace I give to you; not as the world gives do I give to you. Let not your heart be troubled, neither let it be afraid... In the world you will have tribulation; but be of good cheer, I have overcome the world."* (John 14:27, 16:33b)

This was the peace that Yun came to know so well during his time in prison.

When Yun returned home, no one was expecting him. The authorities had not informed the family of his release, so Deling was utterly astonished to open the door and to see her husband standing outside. She woke up little Isaac, now four years old, and brought him to his father.

Isaac recalls,

"When I was four years old, my mother woke me in the middle of the night and said, 'Isaac, wake up, your father has come home.' My first reaction to her words was: 'Mother, what is a father?' In school I had learned something about family and I had heard about fathers, but I didn't know what the real meaning of the

51

word was. I went out into the yard and saw a man standing there. 'Who is that?' I asked myself.
My mother said to me, 'Isaac, this is your father, call him father.' I thought to myself, 'No! I can not call anyone a father whom I do not know.' At that moment I did not know how to respond, so I hid behind my mother and didn't say a word to the man in the yard."

Over the following days, Isaac gradually warmed up to his father and, for the first time, their family was all together under one roof.

Three days after returning home, Yun received a strange dream from the Lord. In it he saw a crowd of Christians chasing him. He was carrying a bright light that the people were trying to get from him. He tried to hide it under his clothes, but the light would shine right through, and the people kept on chasing him.

When he told Deling about the dream, she said, "The authorities are using you like a light to attract moths. They let you out of prison so that when believers come to you, they can arrest them. The Lord is telling us that it is too difficult to hide you from the believers."

Two weeks later a government meeting took place, and it was announced that Yun was under strict surveillance and would have to write a monthly report on all of his activities. He even had to ask the police for permission if he wanted to leave his village.

At first he did not want to write the reports and tried to justify his decision by citing the time when the Lord told Peter to obey God and not man, but the Lord corrected him with these words, *"Submit yourselves to every ordinance of man for the Lord's sake... For this is the will of God, that by doing good you may put to silence the ignorance of foolish men."* (1 Peter 2:13, 15)

For the next two years, Yun faithfully filled out his monthly reports to the police, using every opportunity to share the gospel with them. Rather than to give details about where he had gone and what he had done, his reports contained what the Lord had taught him in the Bible during the past month.

June 4, 1989, was a pivotal day for the house churches. On that day, hundreds of (some reports say up to 3,000) students were brutally gunned down by the Chinese military in what is known in the West as the Tiananmen Square massacre. What had initially been a peaceful protest by university students, attempting to push their government to reform, degraded into violence as the government came down hard on them with tanks and troops.

This heavy-handed approach to handling dissents caused disillusionment among many people groups across China, particularly in the intellectual classes. Blind faith in Communism and Marxist ideology began to be questioned, and more people began to desire spiritual truth.

Up to that time, most Christians were poor farmers, and the revival was largely limited to farming communities in the poorest areas of China (among uneducated people). From 1989 on, the revival started to spread among even students and government workers. The gospel was moving through big cities, bringing salvation to the multitudes wherever it was proclaimed!

In Yun's village alone, several Communist Party members left the Party, committed their lives to Christ, and began to proclaim the good news. Even those who had persecuted Yun's family while he was in prison repented and became strong servants of the Lord.

The police couldn't deny the sudden increase in miracles and conversions in the town, but they were powerless to stop them. They recognized some mysterious power at work and were afraid to touch the believers. In those days, the police mostly stayed inside their stations instead of harassing the Christians.

The multitudes of new believers needing discipleship were too numerous for the handful of Christian leaders to deal with. They were so busy preaching that they often didn't even have time to eat, let alone to see their own families. Yun and other preachers were constantly traveling from province to province, proclaiming the Good News of Christ and seeing the Lord work great miracles of healings. In some places, people were so desperate to hear God's Word that the preachers had to be carried over the heads of the crowd in order to go to the next meeting.

With such a bountiful harvest and fruitful ministry, Yun and his coworkers began to be not only physically, but also spiritually exhausted. They had almost forgotten the lesson that Jesus gave us by sending the crowds home so that He could go up the mountain to commune with His Heavenly Father.

The leaders realized that intense training programs were needed to disciple new believers and to prepare them to preach to others. They started to hold Bible schools in caves cut into the hillside, in order to fill the need for capable Bible teachers and evangelists. Little did they know at the time that the foundation was being laid for the *Back to Jerusalem* training schools that would one day send thousands of Chinese missionaries out to the nations.

From the time of his release from prison until the middle of 1991, Brother Yun was traveling all over China to preach the gospel. He, and countless other leaders, would wake before dawn to dedicate the day to the Lord and then preach and teach until midnight. The leaders soon realized that they were starting to get worn down.

In early 1991, Yun realized he had burned out, but he still refused to rest. The Lord warned him that he had become too busy and had left his first love. The demands of ministry were so great that he was in danger of putting the ministry before his family and even God. How tempting it can be to become caught up in this precious work and to forget about the God who made it all possible!

That May, a wave of persecution came over the house churches. One night, Deling awoke terrified from a dream and insisted that they flee their home immediately. When asked what happened, she said that the Lord was warning them to leave: "Yun, the Lord has showed me that if you don't obey His leading, you will be taken to a place you don't want to go to. Let's leave now, while it's still dark, so we can get away without being seen."

Yun tried to reason with her, saying that they needed to care for the wheat harvest that was coming and should wait a few days before leaving. She told him that he had become too stubborn and unreceptive to the counsel of others. Even the Lord urged him to leave, but he refused to listen.

The years of phenomenal success in ministry had planted a seed of pride in Yun's heart. He began to make decisions based on his own wisdom and logic, rather than obeying the Lord. He was in desperate need of a break, and the Lord was about to give it to him.

Four days after Deling's dream, he was arrested outside their home. His disobedience and pride led not only to his arrest, but that of his wife and coworkers as well. Since he refused to rest and to develop his personal relationship with the Lord, God was putting him in a place where he could no longer be distracted. We should never forget that God is a jealous God and will not let anything get between Him and His children.

He and a coworker, Brother Chuan, were each sentenced to three years of hard labor and sent to a detention center before being sent to the labor camp.

There, Yun expected to be "welcomed" with severe beatings by the cell leader. It was common for prisoners to do so in order to prove who was boss, but an officer with Christian relatives intervened, and he was mostly spared the beatings. His family was even allowed to visit after a few days.

After five months at the detention center, he was sent to Da'an Prison Labor Camp in northwest Henan. For the first few days he wasn't allowed to speak to anyone, and the other prisoners, suspecting him to be a very bad person, beat him terribly. Yun saw that there were many sick and malnourished prisoners in the camp and sought opportunity to minister to them once he was allowed to speak.

A few months into his sentence, he had convinced the guards that he was a trained masseur, and they allowed him to massage ill inmates while secretly sharing the gospel with them. In this way many prisoners were healed and came to believe in the Lord Jesus Christ. Soon everyone in the camp knew of Yun's faith and of his God who could heal people. The prison director even came to him for help with his sore neck and promoted Yun to cell leader.

His good favor with the camp leadership opened the door for him to work in the library, to edit government reports, and even to select music for broadcasting over the prison loudspeakers. Despite his lack of education, the Lord had given him jobs in the prison that even some inmates with university degrees had been denied. Yun's second prison term was very educational for him, like the kind of Bible school he had really needed.

Although he wasn't allowed to send or to receive mail, the Lord provided a way for him to do so through a lady whose shop was attached to the prison wall. One day Yun had noticed a hymnbook in her shop and soon found out that she attended a Three Self church. Once she realized that he wasn't a dangerous criminal, she did everything she could to help him. She would sometimes prepare delicious food for him and also became a messenger between him and his family and coworkers.

His renown as a masseur reached the ears of the head doctor of the clinic, whose father had been left half-paralyzed by a stroke. Yun admitted that he wasn't trained in massage, but she was desperate for anything to help her father. Her connections allowed her to get permission for him to regularly come to her home and massage her father.

On his first visit, the doctor offered him something to eat, but he said, "Thank you, but I'm fasting and praying that your father will receive a great blessing from the Lord." The doctor's mother overheard him from the other room and burst into tears.

The doctor trusted him enough to leave him alone with her parents while she went back to work. Once alone, Yun told the old man how Jesus had born his sin on the cross and urged him to receive Jesus into his heart so that he could be healed. Soon the couple renounced their sins together and made Jesus the Lord of their lives. Although the old man wasn't healed immediately, Yun knew that their prayers were going to be answered.

The very next morning the old man felt something strike him on his neck and on his back. Afterward he was able to move his head and then rose up on his feet and walked. He had been completely healed!

The doctor told Yun the news and brought him to her home for breakfast that day. Her father told him his testimony and they all thanked the Lord together. As soon as the old man was able to walk up and down stairs, he went out and sought forgiveness from all those he had wronged in the past and shared the gospel with all his friends.

The old man's testimony even reached the secretary of the Prison Labor Camp Political Committee, who had Yun sent to a massage school for professional training. The prison even paid Yun's tuition so that he could improve his skills and be an even greater help to the sick inmates. He spent the day in school and returned to the labor camp at night with stacks of books to read.

Hundreds of people came to him for massages, even high-level Communist Party members, and they all heard the gospel. Some believed it and invited him to their homes so their whole family could hear the wonderful news of eternal life through Jesus Christ.

***

In the meantime, things at home were more difficult than Yun knew. In prison he was always given enough food to survive, but it wasn't so for his family. Yun's daughter Yilin was only seven months old when he was incarcerated. Without anyone to go out and earn wages to feed the family, they were totally destitute.

Usually when someone is put in jail in China, the authorities come and confiscate everything of value in that person's home. This compounds the poverty of the prisoner's family and leaves them without any way to provide for themselves.

While Yun was in prison, the police fined his family a large sum of money for breaking China's one-child policy. Since the family had no money to pay them, the authorities came and destroyed the door of his family's home, locked up his mother without any food, and forced Deling to have an operation that would prevent her from having any more children.

To make matters worse, Isaac was constantly persecuted in school by students and teachers alike, until finally he wasn't able to attend school at all. On a very painful visit to see his father in the labor camp, Isaac wept and said, "My classmates mock me and say you are a dirty criminal who deserves to be in prison. The teacher told the other children that we are stupid because we believe in Jesus." This cut Yun to the heart, but he prayed that it would be a precious time from the Lord for his dear son to learn to love and forgive as Jesus had.

Those who pray for Chinese Christians in prison need to also pray for the prisoners' families. They often suffer even more than their loved ones behind bars.

Seeing his family dressed in rags and reduced to mere skin and bones from lack of food left a deep impression on Yun. He made a commitment to the Lord to do whatever he could to prevent other families of imprisoned Christians from having to suffer the same hardships. Yun still continues to raise financial support for the families of those "living martyrs."

There is a popular teaching in many churches around the world today that God wants to bless His church with wealth and prosperity. This teaching is not only missing from the pages of Scripture, but the testimony of Brother Yun and the Chinese church proves it to be an utter farce. In fact, coming to Jesus for wealth is the equivalent of elevating the gifts above the Giver. The Bible gives one example after another of people suffering for their faith, and church history is written with the blood of those who gave their lives out of love for Jesus. Rather than looking for riches in this life, Jesus tells us:

"Do not lay up for yourselves treasures on earth, where moth and rust destroy and where thieves break in and steal; but lay up for yourselves treasures in heaven, where neither moth nor rust destroys and where thieves do not break in and steal. For where your treasure is, there your heart will be also." (Matthew 6:19-21)

CHAPTER 7

By God's grace, Yun was released from Da'an Prison Labor Camp one year early, after only serving 19 months there. He walked out of the prison on May 25, 1993, to find a loving wife waiting for him at the gate.

Almost immediately upon his return, requests for Yun to preach started pouring in from all over. Yun had learned from his past mistakes and decided to first pray with his wife and seek God's will for their ministry together. If his second time in prison had taught him one thing, it was to never abandon his family for ministry.

The pitiful condition of his family when they visited him in prison was something Yun would never forget. His second imprisonment became a crossroads in his marriage. He realized that he had been ignoring his family for too long. Even when not in prison, he was rarely home to see his family, and Deling had to hold the household together all by herself. He felt the Lord warning him that he would lose his family if he didn't repent and make them a top priority in his life.

From that point forward Yun would make a serious effort to instruct Chinese church leaders not to sacrifice their families for the ministry. He encouraged leaders to take their families with them while on preaching trips and to even make them part of their ministries.

He emphasized the fact that one who does not properly care for his own family cannot possibly be an effective shepherd in the church of God (1 Timothy 3:5). In the life of a Christian, God must always come first, family second, and ministry third. Unfortunately several house church leaders opposed Yun in this teaching, and the problem of leaders choosing ministry over family continues to be one of the major weaknesses of the Chinese house churches today.

After a week of prayer and fasting, God spoke to Yun through one of Jesus' parables found in the gospel of Matthew:

"Then the kingdom of heaven shall be likened to ten virgins who took their lamps and went out to meet the bridegroom. Now five of them were wise, and five were foolish. Those who were foolish took their lamps and took no oil with them... And while they went to buy, the bridegroom came, and those who were ready went in with him to the wedding; and the door was shut. Afterward the other virgins came also, saying, 'Lord, Lord, open to us!' But he answered and said, 'Assuredly, I say to you, I do not know you.'" (Matthew 25:1-3, 10-12)

For Yun, this parable emphasized the critical importance of making sure the followers of Christ in China had their spiritual lamps full of oil at all times.

The Bible often represents the Holy Spirit as oil, so these verses emphasized the need for everyone in the house churches to be full of the Spirit and to take the presence of the Lord with them wherever they went. So much time had been spent on evangelism that there had been little time for true discipleship, and Yun now clearly saw the next step that the Lord wanted him to take: establishing "Oil Stations" where Christian workers could be trained for the ministry.

He met with other leaders, and they readily agreed. After prayer, they selected thirty young believers for a two-month training session that would be held in a cave on top of a mountain. This was to be the first Oil Station and they decided to call it the "Prophet Samuel Training Center."

The school centered mainly on internalizing God's Word through meditation on, and memorization of, the Bible. Each student had to read through the whole New Testament and memorize a chapter every day. Having large portions of Scripture committed to memory meant that no one could take God's Word away from them, even if every Bible were confiscated or they were locked in prison for years without access to one. It was the verses that Yun had memorized that kept him alive on many occasions in prison, and he wanted to make sure that the next generation of persecuted Christians would be even better prepared.

The training center relied solely on the support of the house churches, so food and other provisions were often scarce. Rather than being discouraged by constant hunger, the evangelists understood that they were being prepared to serve in the poorest and neediest areas, where everyone was in a similar condition.

On January 16, 1994, after the laying on of hands by the church elders, the first team of workers was sent out into the field. They were sent to locations all over China, with a particular focus on the areas that had been least reached with the gospel.

As the training center began to grow, the Lord moved in the hearts of some Christians in the West who started providing funds for the work. Since the house churches were barely able to support themselves at the time, God used the abundance of the West to provide for the needs of this new army of Chinese missionaries. This established a precedent of likeminded Westerners providing support for God's work in China without trying to interfere with the work itself.

Many around the world saw that God had clearly used the communist revolution to clear the sometimes-overbearing Western Christians out of China, in order to prepare the way for a unique church led by Jesus alone. The time had come for foreigners to support their Chinese brothers and sisters as equals and partners in ministry.

One Scandinavian brother put it best when he said to Yun, "We haven't come to China to dominate your work or to control anything. Nor have we come to impose our own agenda or to build beautiful church buildings. We submit ourselves to the vision God has given to the house churches, and we want to serve you in any way we can to see that vision become a reality."

Another ministry that the Lord led Yun to start was for the many pregnant Christian women who were under pressure to have abortions. The government often forced women to abort their second child in order to follow China's one-child law. Even to this day, many families with more than one child must pay enormous fines to the government, and those children are often denied basic health care and education. Christian women in prison or with families in prison were often forced to have abortions as well.

The Bible teaches that life is precious and people are created in the image of God. The atheistic message taught around the world today is that unborn children are only clumps of cells undergoing chemical changes and cannot be considered human. This thinking has justified the mass murder of countless millions of unborn babies every year.

God called the prophets Isaiah and Jeremiah to their ministries while they were still in their mothers' wombs (Isaiah 49:1, Jeremiah 1:5). How could God call to His service a mere handful of cells?

The Bible also tells us that God forms us in the womb and we are "fearfully and wonderfully made" (Psalm 139:13-16). Therefore it is an abominable sin to have an abortion, and Yun had a deep burden in his heart to save the lives of as many children as possible. Yun committed himself to finding Christian homes that could raise each baby that was at risk of being aborted and provided a refuge for these children in his own home until the time that a permanent home could be found for them.

It often took time to find families willing to receive the infants, so sometimes there were up to eleven children in Yun's home. He kept bringing home more and more babies, but the Lord provided for them, and eventually they were all sent to loving Christian families. Over time, many churches began to follow Yun's example and started caring for orphans and abandoned children.

During this time God also placed in Yun and Deling's heart the desire to unite the Chinese house churches. The movement that had began in the 1970s as a single, unified work of God had become fractured into several different networks that often shunned fellowship with each other.

One reason for this was an influx of doctrinally biased materials coming in from other countries. Originally, foreign Christian organizations had only focused on sending Bibles into China, but over time many gradually started sending in other materials of a divisive nature. These reading materials contained largely denominational theology, and through them the factional nature of the Western church was reintroduced to the Chinese. Financial gifts provided by those who sent the books also lured many leaders off the path of unity.

The house churches began to split up according to which Western organization had offered them support. Leaders began to separate over newfound doctrinal differences, and churches started to speak evil of each other. In a very short time, the house churches had been separated into ten or twelve different networks, many of which exist to this day.

As the situation worsened and division spread among the churches, Yun and his wife set out to bring people back together under the banner of the love of Jesus Christ. Having learned his lesson, Yun now took Deling with him everywhere he went to establish new training centers and to foster unity in the house churches.

Over the next two years, many of the top leaders in the various house church networks agreed to unify, and barriers to fellowship started to break down. Many of these men had been close to each other in the past and had endured suffering in prison together during previous times of intense persecution. For them, uniting was reestablishing old bonds. The younger leaders under them, however, didn't have such experiences and were often opposed to unifying with groups they didn't know.

In October 1996, the senior leaders of five house church networks were elected to be the first elders of the unity movement, which they named "Sinim Fellowship" after a verse in the Bible in which "Sinim" is believed to refer to China, *"Surely these shall come from afar; Look! Those from the north and the west, and these from the land of Sinim."* (Isaiah 49:12)

The following month Sinim elders had their first meeting. Many repented for the animosity they had harbored against others in their hearts, and God continued to break down barriers. They realized that their theological differences were centered on nonessential issues and were not justifiable grounds for division.

At a meeting four years later, the leaders estimated how many believers were in each of their networks. The combined total came to 58 million.

At another meeting of house church leaders in March 1997, something unexpected happened that would lead to many changes in Yun's life. A Chinese-American sister, who had been invited to attend the meeting, was followed to the meeting place by government agents.

By the time Yun arrived, several of the other leaders had already been arrested and taken away. He had no idea he was walking into a trap. Upon entering the apartment where the meeting was to take place, Yun and those with him were greeted by armed police officers pointing guns at them. Yun tried to escape by jumping out the window, but about a dozen police were waiting outside.

The officers pounced on him immediately and began stomping on him with their steel-toed boots and whipping him with their pistol handles. All he could do was to curl up on the ground and ask Jesus to give him strength. After they started shocking him with electric batons, he lost consciousness.

Once they had been placed in a holding cell, Yun and his coworkers found out that the order for their arrest had come all the way from the central government in Beijing. The national authorities were afraid that the house churches would unite and form an opposition party against the government. Satan used every means possible to prevent unity in God's church in China.

Yun and the others were tied together and beaten mercilessly with batons and sticks. They expected to be taken out and executed at any moment.

Police were also sent to Yun's hometown to collect evidence against him. They ended up arresting his wife and around 120 other believers who were worshiping together at the time. Deling was then sent to prison.

At Yun's hearing, the judge asked him whether he would escape if he had the chance. Yun gave an honest reply by saying that he must obey the calling that God has placed on his life and would do whatever it took to continue preaching the gospel all over China.

The enraged judge swore that he would make sure Yun could never get away, "I am going to break your legs permanently, so you'll never escape again!"

He ordered Yun to be sent to an interrogation room. There several guards forced him to sit on the floor with his legs apart. They then proceeded to beat his knees and feet fiercely with batons. He was beaten until his legs below the knee turned completely black and lost all feeling.

Yun was beaten and questioned non-stop for almost two days straight. Throughout the beatings he was denied food and water. The interrogators would even rotate shifts, so they could keep on beating him without exhausting themselves.

He later recalled,

"I began to pray for death. I begged the Lord to take me home. It became my strongest desire to die, but let me warn you, it is not easy to die if you have a calling on your life. You can pray for it. You can plead for it. You might even seek for it in places where it is easily found, but you won't find it. Remember this warning. Today I am so glad that God does not answer all of my foolish prayers."

Without his Bible, Yun relied on the verses he had memorized to give him peace and hope. His situation seemed hopeless, but he was greatly encouraged by God's promises, such as Psalm 27:1-3, *"The LORD is my light and my salvation; whom shall I fear? The*

*LORD is the strength of my life; of whom shall I be afraid?
When the wicked came against me to eat up my flesh, my
enemies and foes, they stumbled and fell. Though an army may
encamp against me, my heart shall not fear; though war may
rise against me, in this I will be confident."*

Yun did his best to appear strong on the outside, but he
was crumbling inside. When the officers told him that he
would probably be sentenced to life in prison, he complained
to God, even accusing Him of failing to protect His people.
Soon he would realize that God had not forsaken him and the
three other brothers imprisoned with him.

Because his legs had been rendered completely
inoperative, guards and other prisoners had to carry Yun
everywhere, whether to the toilet or to the torture room. This
allowed him brief but precious moments of fellowship with
other pastors and leaders who were often made to carry him.

One guard that frequently carried him turned out to be
from a Christian family. Although he would beat Yun as his
job required, he showed mercy by only beating him in a way
that would cause minimal damage to his body.

Despite the fact that Yun was unable to walk, the prison
authorities were still afraid that he would escape. They placed
a fake prisoner in Brother Xu's cell in order to spy on Yun.
One day this informant became seriously ill and the guards
allowed Yun to massage him. Brother Xu prayed while Yun
massaged the man. Within minutes he was completely healed.
After this incident the guards often came to Yun for massages
and started to treat him better.

Although the government had sent this man, who
pretended to be a Christian in order to spy on the pastors, the
Lord used the situation to provide Yun with a Bible. The
informant had been given a Bible in order to make him look
like an authentic Christian, but he never read it and didn't
mind if Yun borrowed it. Yun was then able to encourage the
other brothers in prison by writing out a few verses on scraps
of paper and secretly passing them on.

Yun remembers that time as the lowest point in his life. His legs were irreparably broken, his wife was also in jail, and he had no idea what had happened to his children. Everything seemed hopeless, but God was about to perform the most amazing miracle yet.

CHAPTER 8

The following account is of the event in Yun's life that has caused the most controversy worldwide. Along with the testimony of his 74-day fast, this miracle has been questioned by many who simply cannot believe in the amazing power of God. The Bible says, *"Jesus Christ is the same yesterday, today, and forever."* (Hebrews 13:8) This means that the same Jesus who healed countless cripples, cast out countless demons, and opened the eyes of countless blind men is the same Jesus who is working in His church today.

Jesus also promised us, *"Most assuredly, I say to you, he who believes in Me, the works that I do he will do also; and greater works than these he will do, because I go to My Father."* (John 14:12)

You will now read about one of those great works that took place in the 20th century inside a maximum-security prison.

Brother Yun's spirit, along with his legs, had been crushed:

"Sitting in the prison, I had lost all vision for the future. I was ready to see my Lord and King. I was done with this world and felt that I had done my task and completed my job. I began to pray for the Lord to take my life because I was ready to leave all the sorrow and pain behind. I felt a strong desire to leave the prison, leave the beatings, leave the pain, and take on my new body and see my King with my own eyes."

However, God wasn't finished using Yun yet. He wanted to show His awesome power both to those who mocked Him and to those who were suffering for His name.

On the evening of May 4, 1997, Yun propped his legs up against the wall like he had done every night since the severe beatings that crippled him. Doing so allowed his legs to go numb so that he didn't feel sharp pain and was able to sleep.

The next morning he awoke with the words of Hebrews 10:35 on his mind, *"Therefore do not cast away your confidence, which has great reward."* God was telling him not to give up hope.

Yun started to read the book of Jeremiah from the Bible that he had borrowed from the other inmate. Jeremiah's words fit his situation so perfectly that it was as if they jumped right off the page: *"Woe is me, my mother, that you bore me, a man of strife and contention to the whole land! I have not lent, nor have I borrowed, yet all of them curse me."* (Jeremiah 15:10 ESV)

As Yun read those words, he wept and cried out to the Lord, "Lord Jesus, just like Jeremiah said, everyone strives against me and curses me. I can't take any more. I've reached the end of myself."

As he continued to complain to God because of his suffering, the Lord humbled him and gave him hope with these words, *"Therefore thus says the LORD: 'If you return, Then I will bring you back; you shall stand before Me; if you take out the precious from the vile, you shall be as My mouth. Let them return to you, but you must not return to them. And I will make you to this people a fortified bronze wall; and they will fight against you, but they shall not prevail against you; for I am with you to save you and deliver you,' says the LORD. 'I will deliver you from the hand of the wicked, and I will redeem you from the grip of the terrible.'"* (Jeremiah 15:19-21)

After reading those verses, the Lord gave Yun another powerful vision. His wife was sitting next to him and caring for his wounds. He turned to her and asked her, "Have I been released?"

She answered, "Why don't you open the iron door?" With that the vision ended.

The Lord then spoke clearly to him, "Now is the time of salvation for you. Stand up and walk out of this prison."

Yun understood that God was telling him to escape but questioned in his heart, "This is a top security prison. You don't walk out of places like this."

The Lord again spoke to him, "Your prison is real, but I am the Truth, and the Truth will set you free."

Brother Xu was held in the cell next to Yun's, and they had arranged to knock on the wall twice as a signal if either of them needed urgent prayer. Yun knocked and Xu began to pray. While praying, Xu found that his cell had been miraculously unlocked. He opened the door and peered into the hallway. There weren't any guards around!

Xu came over to Yun's cell and told him urgently, "You must escape!" and then went to the toilet. After returning he repeated the command, "Yun, you *must* escape!"

Such an idea sounded like pure insanity, considering the tight security of the prison. Yun's cell was on the third floor of the prison, each floor having an iron gate at the end of the corridor that could only be opened from the outside. Each of these gates regularly had an armed guard stationed on each side, two guards for each gate. This means that escape would require a walk through three locked iron gates and by six armed guards just to get the inmate to the prison courtyard.

Further complicating the situation, Yun hadn't been able to walk in over six weeks! Though tempted to believe in his own logic, Yun remembered the words of Christ, *"With men this is impossible, but with God all things are possible."* (Matthew 19:26)

God had clearly spoken to him through the Bible verses that morning, through the vision, and through Brother Xu. He knew that not to act would be disobedience. Past experience had taught him that when God clearly speaks, it is not a time for discussion and debate about what to do; it is a time for immediate action according to what God has said. The more impossible a task may seem, the more simple faith and blind obedience is called for.

"True obedience is to receive and obey something that is totally impossible," says Yun.

71

It was about eight o'clock in the morning on May 5, 1997. Logically speaking, it was the worst time attempt an escape because all the guards were alert and at their posts. Yun pulled on his pants and was amazingly able to stand on his own two feet! He wouldn't realize it until hours later, but the Lord had instantly healed both of his legs.

Praying under his breath, he slowly walked toward the iron gate at the end of the hall. The only way to open the gate was by pushing a button on the outside, where the guards were posted. The gate remained shut until the very moment that Yun reached it. It happened that another Christian, Brother Musheng, was just being returned to his cell after sweeping the prison courtyard. The guard opened the gate for him just as Yun approached it, so that Yun could walk straight through before it closed. It was another miracle of the Lord's timing!

Brother Musheng would later say about that event:

"I hadn't seen Yun walk since his legs were broken; in fact, I was one of the three men who had to carry him around in the prison. He couldn't do anything for himself because of his condition, so we even had to wash his clothes for him. As a guard walked me back to my cell that morning, we stopped to be let through the security gate. I couldn't believe it when I saw Yun walking out! He walked right past me, but the guard didn't notice him at all."

The reason why the guard with Brother Musheng didn't notice Yun was because a telephone rang down the hallway the moment he opened the gate. He was running to answer it while Yun calmly walked through the gate.

Yun then proceeded to walk down the stairs to the gate on the second floor. This gate was often left open during the day because a guard was stationed at a desk facing it. As Yun approached the gate, he sensed the Lord telling him, "Go now! The God of Peter is your God!"

Yun walked right past the guard without being noticed. Although the guard was staring straight at him, his eyes didn't even acknowledge Yun's presence. It seemed that the Lord had blinded the guard's eyes for that brief moment.

Expecting to be shot in the back at any second, Yun walked down the last flight of stairs while silently asking the Lord to prepare to receive his spirit. Much to his surprise, the main gate on the first floor was wide open. Even the guards usually posted there were nowhere to be seen!

He walked out into the bright sunlight of the courtyard. There were several guards in the yard, but Yun just walked past them without them even noticing he was there. At the end of the yard was the main gate to the prison—the last barrier to freedom—and it was miraculously ajar!

This was how Brother Yun became the first prisoner to ever escape from Zhengzhou Number One Maximum Security Prison. The vision of iron doors being opened, that the Lord had given to him during his first imprisonment, had been fulfilled.

Brother Musheng later testified, "I climbed to the cell window and watched him cross the yard and disappear through the gate. There were probably thirty guards there at the time, but none of them noticed Yun escape! He even walked right past several of them."

Brother Xu also confirms, "We watched as Yun walked out the front gate of the prison to freedom. I believe that God chose to release Yun in such a manner because the prison authorities had mocked God and Yun by smashing his legs and saying, 'We'd like to see you escape now!' The Lord is always up to meeting a challenge!"

As soon as Yun walked out the front gate, a taxi pulled up and asked him where he wanted to go. He remembered the address of a local Christian family and was soon taken there. The family warmly welcomed him in and said that they had been expecting him.

The day before, the Lord had told the mother of the family, "I will release Yun and the first place he will stop will be at your home. He will stay for a short time and pray with you." God had made all the preparations for him in advance.

The family had prepared clothes and food for him, and they directed him to a secret hiding place that they had arranged for him. As he pedaled on a bicycle through back alleys, to avoid the roadblocks and police checkpoints set up to catch him, he finally realized that his legs had been fully healed.

Soon everyone knew about his escape because it was broadcast on television news, and soldiers from the People's Liberation Army even began a door-to-door search for him. Police dogs were sent out to track his scent, but a sudden storm that began the moment Yun exited the prison completely washed away any trace of him. God had covered his tracks. Yun would remember his escape from prison as the most amazing experience of his life.

At the same time, the Lord had also prepared Yun's wife for the news of his escape. She had been released from prison two weeks earlier. On the day of Yun's escape, the Lord showed her in a vision that Yun was indeed free. She immediately got on a bus to Zhengzhou and went to the house of a church leader that Yun would end up visiting that very night.

When they met at the leader's home, they embraced and praised the Lord from Psalm 126:1-3, *"When the LORD brought back the captivity of Zion, we were like those who dream. Then our mouth was filled with laughter, and our tongue with singing. Then they said among the nations, 'The LORD has done great things for them.' The LORD has done great things for us, and we are glad."*

Because his escape was such an embarrassment to the authorities, they made every effort to apprehend him, even sending spies into house church meetings to ask for his whereabouts. Because he had become such a security risk, churches were afraid to invite him to speak. For the first time in Yun's life, it appeared that every possible door for ministry in China was shut to him.

Yun had always struggled with an inclination to find his source of joy in ministry, instead of finding his sole satisfaction in God alone, so through this situation God removed that idol from his heart. God also taught Yun the importance of simply resting in God, rather than always working for God.

Little did he know that a new chapter in his life was about to begin. While recovering from an illness in the hospital, the Lord told him, "I will send you to a new place. You won't understand their language at all. There will be many strange faces before you, but I command you to go there and to awaken those people!"

At another time, while he was meditating on Scripture, Yun was reminded of what God commanded Paul in Acts 22:18, "Make haste and get out of Jerusalem quickly, for they will not receive your testimony concerning Me."

The Lord seemed to keep saying to him, "Your witness for Me in China is complete. People are too frightened to accept your ministry. You must leave China."

God's new direction for his life was again confirmed by the phone call of a friend. This man told Yun that fleeing China was the next stage in the fulfillment of God's calling for him, since childhood, to take the gospel to the west and to the south. After talking it over with Deling, Yun was finally convinced that it was time to flee.

Although Yun had no passport, and it was impossible for convicted criminals to apply for them, the Lord provided one for him through a Chinese businessman. This man risked his own safety by giving his passport to Yun, but there was still a problem: the man's passport photo looked nothing like Yun! Nevertheless, by faith they purchased a one-way ticket from Beijing to Frankfurt, Germany scheduled to depart on September 28, 1997.

As the departure date approached, they sought the Lord's guidance and protection fervently. If there had been any sense of warning or doubt about leaving, Yun would have immediately cancelled his plans. On the contrary, those who were praying for him kept giving him encouraging words that confirmed his decision.

On the morning of Yun's departure, the Lord gave him a strong warning, "When you enter the customs hall at the airport, say only what I instruct you to say." It was these instructions that would later save him.

After filling out the necessary customs forms, Yun entered the line for document inspection. When the officer looked at Yun and the passport he gave him, he laughed because it didn't look like Yun at all. He showed the other officers the passport and they laughed as well. Yun was asked to step aside while the officer took the passport to a back office and confirmed that it wasn't his.

Amazingly, though the passport clearly did not belong to Yun, the officer stamped the passport and let him through, saying, "There's no way you will get permission to enter Germany. They'll just send you back on the next flight!"

Within a few minutes, Yun was on a plane to Germany and out of the clutches of the Chinese authorities. Against impossible odds, God had freed him once again!

Upon his arrival in Germany, the customs officers inspected his passport and shook their heads. They could easily tell that it didn't belong to him, but Yun stood his ground and simply stared them in the eyes with a stern face. By yet another work of God's grace, they stamped Yun's passport and allowed him entry into the country.

As he set foot on German soil for the first time, the Holy Spirit spoke powerfully to him, "In the same way that I brought you out of prison and out of China, so shall I bring one hundred thousand of my children out of China to be my witnesses throughout Asia." God was reaffirming to Yun His calling on the Chinese house churches to fulfill the *Back to Jerusalem* vision.

Yun applied for refugee status with the German government, but at first they didn't believe his stories. Soon German Christians, who had worked with him in China, came and proved his identity and the truth of all he had been through.

Yun was sent to a refugee detention center and then to the hospital where doctors discovered he had severe lung damage, undoubtedly caused by guards stomping on his chest while he was in prison. Like Paul and countless Christians before him, Yun bore on his body the marks of the Lord Jesus.

A few years later, Yun was to find out why the Lord had instructed him not to say anything at the airport in Beijing. An employee of a European security company informed him that they had installed voice-detecting microphones and software at that airport. If Yun had spoken a single word, the computers would have immediately matched his voice with recordings the police had on file, and he would have been arrested on the spot!

God had worked miracle after miracle to send His chosen servant out of China, with the express purpose of building cooperation between the Chinese and Western churches for taking the gospel to the ends of the earth.

CHAPTER 9

Yun's family had also endured much during his third imprisonment and during the time after his escape from China. With both Yun and Deling in prison, Christian friends had to hide their two children from the government. The children of prisoners in China are often taken by the state and brainwashed to hate their "criminal" parents and to love the communist system. Police were searching for them in Nanyang, so Isaac and Yilin had to be relocated to the capital of Henan, Zhengzhou. When things started becoming dangerous there, they were moved to faraway Shandong Province.

Yun's son Isaac tells about that difficult time as follows:

When I was twelve years old, my father was arrested for the third time, and a few days later my mother also went to prison. My sister was only seven years old at the time. The local churches were afraid to take us in because the police were looking everywhere for us. We were finally taken in by a community in another city. There we called people we did not know before "father" and "mother," so no one noticed anything.

For two years, I was often on the street and searched garbage dumps for items to sell so I could buy something to eat for my sister and I. At that time I often hated God because I could not understand him.

I asked him, "God, why did you let all this happen? My grandparents believed in you and were often dragged through the streets wearing tall white hats with 'anti-communist' written on them. My parents believed in you, and they were arrested again and sentenced to many years in prison. My sister and I have also believed in you, and now we have lost our home and our parents! Jesus, what kind of God are you?'

I could not understand God with my own religious way of thinking. How could I understand why God just took away everything from me? My heart was bitter. At the time, I said to God: "When I grow up, I will pursue anything except what my father does. I'll never succeed with my father's God."

But I learned over time that as a father cares for his children, so God takes care of us. Though we may hate Him, He'll never hate us. We sometimes do not like Him much, but He loves us all the time. God is faithful and patient. It feels so good to have him as a Father in my life.

After Yun's escape to the West, his family members were in constant peril until arrangements could be made for them to leave China as well. The children learned the life of the cross from a very young age.

Six months after his arrival in Germany, Yun was granted refugee status and began to seek wisdom from the Lord about how to bring his family out of China. In 1999 they made the long journey through southwest China and were subsequently smuggled into Myanmar (Burma). They planned to lay low in Myanmar until all the papers were in order for their entry to Germany. When the time was right, they would cross the border into Thailand and board a plane to Germany with the same refugee status that Yun had received.

The process ended up taking much longer than they had hoped, so Deling and the children settled down in Myanmar for the time being. Isaac and Yilin enrolled in a local school and began to learn Burmese. After a few months, Yun was able to visit them, and the family had their first Christmas together in thirteen years. A friend had secured Burmese ID cards for them, so they thought they could freely travel around the country; however, the cards later turned out to be fake.

In February 2001, after a two-year wait, all the preparations were completed for the family to leave. Yun once again flew to Myanmar in order to send them off to the Burmese-Thai border. Their intention was for Deling and the children to make an overland crossing into Thailand, while Yun flew on ahead to meet them there. Nothing went according to plan.

Two days before their intended departure, Yun had another dream. In it he saw himself leaving Myanmar with his family. Isaac went on ahead and crossed safely, but just as Yun was about to pass through customs, he was stopped by an officer. The man had seen Yun's Burmese ID card when he opened his bag for inspection. In the dream, the officer sent Yun to the interrogation room. At this point, he suddenly regained consciousness.

They all agreed that the dream was a warning from the Lord and that they needed to be careful and seek the Lord's protection while making their final preparations. Deling urged Yun to give her his ID card, so he wouldn't get into trouble.

Expecting everything to go as smoothly as planned, Yun ignored the dream and the advice of his wife. Rather than trusting in the Lord, Yun assumed that his German passport would protect him from any difficulties. Unfortunately, he was mistaken.

When the time came to leave, Yun recognized the inside of the airport from his dream. As he walked through customs, the exact same officer from his dream looked at his passport, ordered him to open his bags, and discovered the fake ID card inside one of the bags. Immediately a serious expression came over the man's face and he sent Yun over to an interrogation room.

It turned out that a war had just broken out between the Burmese government and a rebel group. Since Yun couldn't speak Burmese or English and had a fake ID card, they assumed that his German passport was also fake, and he must be a rebel spy.

The war caught Isaac by surprise as well. No sooner had his plane landed near the Thai border than gunfire and artillery shelling began all around the area. The airport where Isaac landed was completely cut off for weeks, and there was no way that he could contact his mother and sister. The original plan had been for the three of them to meet at the border, and then to cross into Thailand together. However, this plan became impossible as soon as the war broke out, since tight restrictions were immediately enforced at all border crossings. Isaac would later recall having to make the journey to the shore of Thailand in a small boat, under gunfire.

As Yun sat alone in the interrogation room at the airport, he repented of his pride and disobedience. The past few years of busy traveling and speaking engagements in the West had worn him out and made him dull to the leading of the Holy Spirit. This was the second time he was imprisoned for trusting in his own strength. God's principles are unchanging, and anyone who disobeys them is guaranteed to fall into trouble.

Yun's inability to speak English or Burmese only angered his interrogators more, so they handcuffed him and made him stand on one leg for a total of about 30 hours. As he stood there, they continually kicked him and beat him with long sticks. Yun was once again reduced to a bruised and bloody mess. As in the past, Yun was able to endure the pain by focusing on what Jesus suffered to pay for our sins. Yun recognized a major difference between his pain and that of Jesus. Jesus was beaten because He obeyed the Lord, while Yun was being beaten for disobeying Him.

While all of this was going on, Yun had no idea that his wife and daughter were still in Myanmar and would have to go to Thailand by a different route. Because of Yun's arrest, the authorities knew their names and were searching for them. Their only option at this point was to get as close to the border as possible by private transportation, and then they would have to cross the mountains into Thailand on foot.

Smugglers helped the family across the mountains barefoot, because the sound of squeaking shoes would alert the border guards. On a moonless night they had to trudge through the jungle, slipping in mud and cutting their feet on jagged rocks.

As they stumbled in the darkness, the Lord reminded Deling of Isaiah 30:20-21, *"And though the Lord gives you the bread of adversity and the water of affliction, yet your teachers will not be moved into a corner anymore, but your eyes shall see your teachers. Your ears shall hear a word behind you, saying, "This is the way, walk in it," whenever you turn to the right hand or whenever you turn to the left."*

Deling noticed that whenever they were about to get lost in the darkness, a light would appear before them and guide them in the right direction. They arrived in Thailand after six long hours of walking. Eventually they were able to meet up with Isaac in Chiang Mai, and together the three of them flew to Germany. After many a trial, the Lord had safely brought them to freedom. Yun's path back to freedom, however, would be a longer one.

Christians around the world were quickly alerted of his arrest and began praying for him. Everyone's greatest concern was that he might be handed over to the Chinese government, which would most certainly execute him.

Representatives of the Chinese government tried to gain access to Yun, but the German embassy intervened, and he was spared. Although they kept trying to find a way to meet him, God prevented the Chinese authorities from ever coming near Yun.

Yun ended up staying in a cell at the airport police station for an entire month while the authorities figured out what to do with him. He used this time as an opportunity to memorize more books of the Bible and draw closer to the Lord.

Yun was then transferred to the largest prison in Myanmar which housed ten thousand prisoners. The situation in this prison was worse than anything Yun had experienced in

China. Many prisoners had AIDS or leprosy, and the smell of rotting flesh and filth permeated the air. Yun was one of one hundred prisoners crammed so tightly into a single cell that they had to lay on their sides to sleep at night.

Even though Yun knew that his imprisonment was the result of his disobedience to the Lord, he could see how desperately the prisoners needed the gospel, and realized that he had been sent there to share it with them.

A predominantly Buddhist nation, Myanmar supplies every prison cell with a Buddhist shrine with an altar for offering prayers. Three times a day the prisoners were forced to sit in Buddhist fashion and meditate while facing the shrine. Through a prisoner who spoke some Chinese, Yun adamantly told the guards that he was a Christian pastor and would never bow down to idols.

During the meditation times, Yun would sing a simple tune to the Lord that touched the hearts of many inmates. Some of them began to sing along with Yun, "Hallelujah..." having no idea what they were singing.

He also discovered that there was a Christian chapel on the premises where Christians could go when the other prisoners were praying to Buddha. An increasing number of inmates, even a Buddhist monk, shortly began to follow him to the chapel in order to hear him sing. God was gathering people around Yun so that he could proclaim the gospel to them.

Because everyone in the prison had to purchase their own food and basic necessities, a great deal of them were starving. The foreign prisoners were periodically taken to another location for questioning and then allowed to buy some items before returning to the prison. Yun used these opportunities to purchase toothbrushes, soap, and large bags of food for his cell mates. If he couldn't verbally communicate God's love to the prisoners, at least he could demonstrate it to them with generosity.

Conflicting reports about Yun's case made him realize that he could only trust in God for the outcome. He understood that God had a purpose for him in the prison and wouldn't let him leave until it had been accomplished.

Unsanitary conditions allowed for diseases to spread quickly throughout the prison. Yun was infected with an awful parasite that made him itch all over and rendered him unable to digest solid food for an entire month. At times he could even see the worms crawling around under the surface of his skin. Yun became so weak from the sickness that he lost consciousness for five days and was hospitalized.

Soon afterward the court issued his sentence: seven years. His Burmese friends were crushed by the news, but he knew that God was with him and actually thanked the judge for allowing him to stay in the country for seven more years. With a wave of his hand, the judge sent him back to the prison hospital.

There were five other Chinese men in the prison, from Singapore and Taiwan, who were serving life sentences for drug smuggling. When they heard that there was a Chinese pastor in the prison's hospital, they feigned illness in order to be sent there.

Yun was greatly moved by the hopelessness in their eyes and told them of the freedom they could have in Jesus, "I've come to tell you that Jesus Christ is the true and eternal Judge. He offered His life for you and is able to forgive you for all of your sins." They wanted to know more, but the guards soon made them return to their cells.

Yun noticed that all prisoners serving life sentences wore special red uniforms. He decided to ask his lawyer to provide him with some red clothes so that he could speak more freely with the condemned men and not be bothered by the guards.

When he met them again they firmly confessed faith in Jesus Christ. They all prayed together, and Yun baptized them under the faucet in the bathroom sink. He told them, "Some men live free in this life, only to face an eternal prison in hell. You may be spending this life in prison, but your names are now written in heaven and you are truly free!" During Yun's time in prison, the Lord would allow him to lead twelve prisoners to Jesus.

The months that Yun was hospitalized not only gave him a chance to preach to the Chinese prisoners, but he later found out that it also kept him from being transferred to a labor camp in the countryside to serve out the rest of his sentence. The time he spent in the hospital provided more time to those who were working diligently toward his release.

Yun was able to teach many Scriptures to the new Christians through song. Because they were singing in a foreign language, the guards didn't suspect them of studying the Bible and actually enjoyed listening to the songs. Yun did his best to teach the believers all he could because he didn't know how much longer he would be in the prison.

After about a month of imprisonment, the Lord kept directing Yun back to John 12:24-25, *"Most assuredly, I say to you, unless a grain of wheat falls into the ground and dies, it remains alone; but if it dies, it produces much grain. He who loves his life will lose it, and he who hates his life in this world will keep it for eternal life."*

While meditating on these verses, he remembered his past experiences with wheat farming. It usually took a seed of wheat about seven months to grow before it would start to appear above the soil. As he connected these thoughts, he began to comprehend that the Lord was showing him that he would only be in jail for seven months. God wanted Yun to die more to self, so He could bring about more fruit through him.

Shortly after Yun was sentenced, the German embassy petitioned the Myanmar government to be merciful and to allow Yun to leave the country. The German government agreed to pay all expenses to transport him back home. Eventually the request was granted and on the morning of September 18, 2001, Yun was taken to the airport and sent on his way. In accordance with God's perfect timing, he had been in prison for exactly seven months and seven days.

After many years of running, suffering, and separation, Yun was finally united with his family in Germany. God used the dire circumstances in Myanmar to teach them all one last lesson in trusting Him before they began a much more comfortable life in the free world.

Today Yun and Deling travel the world, sharing their testimony about God's mighty work in China and sharing the *Back to Jerusalem* vision that God has given to the Chinese house churches. Their burning desire is to see people of all tongues, tribes, and nations bowing down before the true King of Kings, Jesus Christ Our Lord.

Yun's life provides solid proof that those who are freed from sin through the power of the cross can live like free men and women regardless of their physical circumstances.

Drawing on his many experiences, Yun often speaks these words to audiences around the globe, "It doesn't matter how big the problems are in your life. They are never greater than the power of the salvation of Jesus Christ. Jesus loves you and He will set you free!"

CHAPTER 10

Brother Yun witnessed a great many miracles and mighty acts of God that cannot possibly be included in this brief account of his life. To hear more of his testimony would only require attending one of his many speaking engagements held around the world. However, there is one more event from his life that ought to be shared for the benefit of the reader.

In one Chinese village there was a man who was demon-possessed and had gone completely crazy. He was so dangerous that his family had to keep him handcuffed and chained up inside a cage that they built for him in their living room. He wasn't even able to feed himself because of the chains. The man had lived this animal-like existence for 18 years by the time Yun came to their village.

Upon arrival, Yun proclaimed that Jesus can heal and cast out all demons. The family invited him to their home to test if what he said was true.

Yun recalls,

> We began to walk around the iron bars of that cell in the middle of their living room, and as we were praising the Lord and praying, the demon-possessed man started to tremble and to fight against his chains. I opened the door to the cage a little and said, "Satan, here is the door. Get out!" and the demon went out from him.
>
> In a fraction of a second this man came back to his senses and said, "Mother, Satan has left me. All the demons are gone. You can remove the handcuffs and chains because I'm totally restored."

Unfortunately his family couldn't free him because the local police had ordered them to keep him bound in the cage for the rest of his life. While under the influence of the demons, in years past, he had killed many people and caused havoc throughout the village; so the police couldn't risk letting him go free again.

Yun took authority over the situation and said, "I command you to bring in some tools; we will cut all his chains so that this man can go and report to the police himself." The man had been completely liberated from the demonic power that had controlled him and reduced him to an animal, something that not even the authorities could deny.

In many ways we are all like this man. We have been born with an incurable disease called sin; it holds us captive under its powers and is a ruthless master. Eventually we all realize that—no matter how hard we try—we always make mistakes and fall into one kind of sin or another. The Bible calls this being a slave to sin.

You might be thinking to yourself right now, "Wait a minute! I've done many good deeds and I try my best to live a good life and to help others." This may be true, but our meager attempts at righteousness are so minuscule compared to God's holiness that the Bible says, *"We are all like an unclean thing, and all our righteousnesses are like filthy rags."* (Isaiah 64:6a)

Not only are our "good deeds" not good enough for God, they are even considered sin in His eyes because: *"whatever is not from faith is sin."* (Romans 14:23b)

In fact, *"without faith it is impossible to please [God], for he who comes to God must believe that He is, and that He is a rewarder of those who diligently seek Him."* (Hebrews 11:6)

Like the man in the story, we are all born chained and handcuffed to our sin. This keeps us from being able to know God and from living a truly fulfilling life, but the good news is that Jesus Christ came, was crucified, and rose from the dead so that we can be freed from sin once and for all! *"For the law of the Spirit of life in Christ Jesus has made me free from the law of sin and death."* (Romans 8:2)

Jesus' purpose in coming to this earth was clear: *"The Spirit of the Lord is upon me, because he has anointed me to proclaim good news to the poor. He has sent me to proclaim liberty to the captives and recovering of sight to the blind, to set at liberty those who are oppressed, to proclaim the year of the Lord's favor. "* (Luke 4:18-19 ESV)

As we progress through life and begin to accomplish our goals we eventually realize that we are never satisfied. We may marry the man or woman of our dreams, become independently wealthy, and buy all the things we ever wanted, but in the end there will be only emptiness and disappointment.

King Solomon was the wisest man who ever lived and had everything that a man could want, including endless wealth and hundreds of wives, but after pursuing pleasure with all his heart he finally realized, *"Vanity of vanities, all is vanity. "* (Ecclesiastes 1:2b)

There are two great truths about living life your own way: it will never satisfy you, and there will be eternal punishment in the end. If we remain in our sins, we will inevitably die and face the eternal wrath of God. Apart from God, all is meaningless and will only be taken away from us when we die.

Dear friend, this does not have to be the case! Just as the demon-possessed man was freed from bondage by the power of Jesus Christ, so can you be freed from the clutches of sin and receive forgiveness. Through Jesus alone there is hope, *"For the wages of sin is death, but the gift of God is eternal life in Christ Jesus our Lord. "* (Romans 6:23)

This gift of eternal life and a personal relationship with the Creator of the universe is available to you at this very moment, if you would but repent of your sins and confess Jesus as your Lord and Savior: *"If you confess with your mouth the Lord Jesus and believe in your heart that God has raised Him from the dead, you will be saved. For with the heart one believes unto righteousness, and with the mouth confession is made unto salvation. "* (Romans 10:9-10)

Elvis Presley, known around the world as the "King of Rock and Roll," is one of the most famous singers who ever lived. He had all the fame and fortune that people chase after in life… yet, he was completely depressed. Near the end of his life, he frequently stated that it was miserable being Elvis Presley. He was so despondent, in fact, that he would take large amounts of prescription drugs in an attempt to make his life more tolerable. He killed himself with a drug overdose when he was only 42 years old.

In contrast, you've just read about a man who has faced death many times and has sometimes given up on life itself, but when looking back on those times will confidently say, "God was faithful."

Brother Yun once said, "I'm so thankful that Jesus loves me so much and has never forsaken me. Likewise, He'll never forsake you. We may lose heart and get discouraged, but He is faithful. He knows you and where you are right now. If you are totally lost in your life and come to Jesus, you'll find the way."

Although some of us may be called to endure more than others, everyone who entrusts their life to Jesus will be able to say these same words from experience.

Of course, becoming a Christian does not mean that all of our problems will disappear, and our lives will become easy. The Bible actually promises quite the opposite, *"All who desire to live godly in Christ Jesus will suffer persecution."* (2 Timothy 3:12)

However, for a Christian, suffering has a greater purpose, often to help us to become closer to God and to sin less. Yun's experiences taught him that when suffering and pain increase, our propensity to sin decreases. That concept can clearly be found in 1 Peter 4:1: *"Therefore, since Christ suffered for us in the flesh, arm yourselves also with the same mind, for he who has suffered in the flesh has ceased from sin."*

If we belong to Christ, we know that whatever happens to us is always for our eternal benefit, *"And we know that all things work together for good to those who love God, to those who are the called according to His purpose."* (Romans 8:28)

When we are able to embrace suffering as a friend, to rejoice and be glad when people slander us, and to bless those who curse us, then we are truly free. To be a true disciple of Jesus costs everything, even your own life. Jesus demands nothing less: *"For whoever desires to save his life will lose it, but whoever loses his life for My sake will find it. For what profit is it to a man if he gains the whole world, and loses his own soul? Or what will a man give in exchange for his soul?"* (Matthew 16:25-26)

Brother Yun tells us, "Christianity isn't just an idea. It is the Truth. It doesn't matter who others say Jesus is; you must know who Jesus really is for yourself."

Do you know who Jesus really is? Have you given your life to Him? If you have, you'll surely never regret it.

CHAPTER 11
Beyond "The Heavenly Man"

Throughout this book have been repeated references to the *Back to Jerusalem* vision, and it was defined clearly in the opening pages. Today there is ample unnecessary confusion around the world about what exactly this vision entails. It is important to understand that the *Back to Jerusalem* vision isn't only some vague idea that has become the driving passion of Brother Yun's ministry and the battle cry of millions of Chinese Christians. It is God's special evangelistic calling for the Chinese house churches to take the gospel to every unevangelized people group between China and Jerusalem, from the Great Wall to the Western Wall.

In spiritual terms, this means taking on the most prominent religions in the world and waging an all-out war against the strongholds of Islam, Hinduism, and Buddhism. As can be seen throughout the history of Christianity, this kind of warfare usually results in martyrdom for many of the warriors. This isn't a battle that is fought with guns and bombs, but by humble, broken people who selflessly enter into the darkest places on earth to share God's love and forgiveness.

Although the Chinese house churches have officially sent Brother Yun as a representative of the *Back to Jerusalem* movement to the world, it isn't an idea that started with him. The vision can be traced back to the time before the communist revolution, when God revealed this vision to several unrelated groups of Chinese churches throughout China. Several teams were actually sent out to obey the calling, but the church in China wasn't yet prepared for such a task, and the result was tragic.

In 1995, Yun was able to meet one of the first *Back to Jerusalem* missionaries who were sent westward in the 1940s. While Yun was sharing the vision with believers in central

China, an old man slowly walked to the front of the room, weeping as he came forward.

He said,

I am Simon Zhao, a servant of the Lord. I was one of the leaders of the Back to Jerusalem Band. We marched across China on foot, preaching the gospel in every town and village we passed through.

After many years of hardship, we finally reached Kashgar, in Xinjiang Province, in 1950. While we were waiting for our visas, in order to continue our journey westward, the communist armies took control of the area. We never got to leave China.

All of our leaders were arrested, and five of us were sentenced to forty-five years of hard labor. I'm the only one who survived. I spent 31 years in prison for the sake of the vision to take the Gospel back to Jerusalem.

I had only been married for four months when the Lord called us to this vision, and my wife had just found out she was pregnant. After we were arrested she had a miscarriage in prison. The last time I saw her was from a distance, through the iron bars of my prison cell. She was long dead by the time I was finally released.

You must understand that the way of the cross is the call to shed blood. You must take the Gospel of Jesus Christ to the Muslim nations and all the way back to Jerusalem. Look to the West!

The Chinese house churches understand that the past decades of persecution, suffering, and torture were all a part of God's training for this task. Today thousands of Chinese missionaries are being trained, and hundreds have already gone beyond their borders and begun the work that God has given to them. The vision is alive.

What makes Back to Jerusalem unique?

There are several factors that make the *Back to Jerusalem* vision unique. For one, it is the vision of one of the fastest growing churches in the world. Today China is seeing an estimated 25,000 – 30,000 people PER DAY coming to the Lord. The rapid growth of Christianity in China is on an astronomical scale! The growth of the Chinese underground house churches is not growing because of a clever strategy, a charting system, a focus on funding, or Western influence. It is exploding because of the power of the Holy Spirit and the zealous dedication of farmer-preachers in the countryside or poor factory workers in a crowded urban setting who are laying down their lives out of love and obedience to the Lord.

Back to Jerusalem is unique because it doesn't have a top leader or a figurehead. There isn't a face, a founder, or a visionary who represents the vision. Brother Yun is a representative for *Back to Jerusalem,* but he cannot be considered the exclusive representative. Brother Yun's testimony may sound extraordinary to the outside world, but it is not unique in China. The amazing testimony of Yun's life in China, with miraculous provision by God and honorable dedication of His servant, is a story commonly found throughout China today.

Back to Jerusalem is unique because it isn't owned by any denomination, group, or organization. No one owns the vision. No one can claim exclusive rights to the vision of the Chinese Church—not even the Chinese churches themselves! Even the churches and underground networks who disagree on many things inside China, and are thus unwilling to join together in any other way, find themselves sold out and dedicated to the selfsame task: taking the Gospel of Jesus Christ from China to the rest of the world—all the way back to Jerusalem. No one can claim the rights to, or control over, this vision of *Back to Jerusalem.*

Back to Jerusalem unique in that it doesn't have a headquarters. There is no large, shiny building on a hill overlooking the valley with hundreds of full-time staff shuffling through papers and emails. It doesn't have monthly overhead for administration expenses. Nor is it owned by an organization that is subject to a board, a committee, or an outside entity, controlling which missionaries are allowed to go or which countries should be targeted.

Back to Jerusalem is unique because it is led by the Chinese themselves. For generations, China has been trading with its neighbors (Pakistan, Afghanistan, Vietnam, North Korea, etc). Chinese can be found in virtually every major country, city, and town selling goods or running restaurants and other businesses. Most people do not know this, but Chinese restaurants are extremely successful door openers for the Chinese. In fact, there is more Chinese fast food restaurants in America than there are McDonalds, Burger King, and Kentucky Fried Chicken outlets combined! Over the years, the Chinese working abroad have been stereotyped as Buddhist, Confucian, Taoist, Animist, and most recently (due to Communism) Atheist. However, the Chinese have never been generalized as Christians. This provides the Chinese missionaries a unique opportunity to covertly enter into most countries around the world, especially those countries that are hostile to Christianity.

Finally, *Back to Jerusalem* is unique because the Chinese missionaries are not raising massive amounts of money to go out and preach the Gospel of Jesus Christ. They are investing in platforms that will sustain themselves. They are starting businesses that will provide visas and living expenses, as well as an avenue for sharing the gospel. Today many Chinese evangelists and missionaries are living on less than $100 USD per month. This is a far cry from the typical monthly budget of a Western missionary.

All in all, the *Back to Jerusalem* vision is a viable missionary movement that is already bringing the Good News into places that have been impenetrable for centuries and completely off limits to Westerners.

Central Asia and the Middle East need Jesus Christ. Jesus is calling His disciples to go there. Are you willing to be one of them? Will you support those who are?

AFTERWORD

Official Church & House Church: What's the Difference?

On the 8th day of the 8th month in the year 2008, the world watched as China put on a magnificent display. People from all over the world traveled to Beijing and walked the streets of Wangfujing. At one end of Wangfujing, the amazed tourists could eat a Big Mac at McDonald's, at the other end they were able to get a "bucket meal" at Kentucky Fried Chicken, and everywhere in between they could buy Nike shoes or Levi Strauss blue jeans. As they walked around this area, many Westerners saw something that confused them: a church.

China has long been known as a communist country that persecutes Christians and sends political dissidents to gulags. Jon Halliday and Jung Chang conducted a major study that estimated the total number of Chinese killed under Mao Zedong to be at least 70 million. Images of Bibles and Christian literature being burnt in the streets and of students standing in front of tanks in Tiananmen Square have long been branded in the minds of people around the world.

The image of a church at the end of Wangfujing seems to prove to many visitors that things are changing. Continual news coverage about the economical and social changes in China has begun to change the thinking of outside observers. To a large degree, the Chinese government has been successful in convincing much of the world, as well as many of its own citizens, that China has complete freedom of religion.

Many pastors and evangelists from Europe and America can be seen preaching in China and openly being hosted by government officials. In October 2009, Franklin Graham, the son of famous American evangelist Billy Graham, spoke at a large church of about 12,000 and has since praised China on its increase of freedom for Christians.

It seems conclusive to most people around the world that the modern China is open and religiously tolerant. It also seems that the term "underground," applied to house churches that are illegal in China, is really irrelevant in the country today.

Most companies and retailers in America love to attend the staged shows put on by the communist government, promoting China's so-called "freedoms," so that they can invest in low-wage production in China with a clean conscience. Often cited proof of China's open-arms reception of Christianity is the fact that it prints more Bibles than any other place on earth through Amity Press. Even Daniel Willis of the Bible Society in New Zealand wrote, "Organizations that appealed for funds to smuggle Bibles into China were wasting ninety percent of their donors' money." He argued that resources would be more effectively used if they were placed behind Amity's legal printing of Bibles. Today Amity Press has printed more than 80 million Bibles.

This begs the questions: Why is Brother Yun traveling around the world to raise awareness and support for the underground house churches? What is really the difference, in China, between a legal church and an illegal church?

It is best that leaders from the underground house churches in China explain this difference for themselves. The following interviews were conducted in a clandestine manner, for the safety of everyone involved. The language used is often strong, and what is said is not necessarily true of all official churches in China, but has been the experience of the leadership of the underground house churches.

INTERVIEW # 1

This interview was conducted with a senior leader from a house church network in Henan Province who cares for churches in Guangdong, Guangxi, Yunnan and Guizhou. He also oversees the process of sending missionaries to South East Asia. The interview took place in a car, as we drove from parking lot to parking lot in Humen, China on April 14, 2009.

In America and Europe there are many people who claim that there is growing religious freedom in China. Is this true?

Yes and no. China is a big country and there have been many changes, but some of those changes have only been new ways of expressing old habits.

Can you elaborate? Many people in the West feel that there is freedom for Christians in China, and they cannot understand why the house churches will not register with the government.

This topic is very important to me. I have never discussed this with any foreigner before. We believe that Christians should not get political. We don't want to argue with anyone, and we don't want to get involved in politics. We don't want to be for China what the Roman Catholic Church was in Western history, but we also do not want to have politicians running the church, setting the doctrine, and leading us away from Christ.

The government in China controls the Three-Self Church and has led many people away from the truth. In 1983, when I was living in my hometown in southern Henan Province, there was a surge of persecution toward Christians in China. The government was not able to destroy the church under Mao Zedong, so they tried a different tactic under Deng Xiaoping by attempting to control it instead. Many pastors were arrested. During that time, my older sister, who was a well-known leader in our hometown, was arrested and told to deny Christ. If she would deny Jesus Christ, they promised that she would be released from prison and be given a post in the official church. The first leaders of the Three-Self Church in my area were all people who had denied Jesus Christ. My sister served three years in prison for refusing to deny the name of Jesus.

Many pastors in the Three-Self Church in China are on the government payroll. They are salaried employees. This is not true everywhere of course, but it is true in my hometown (in Henan). If pastors are paid by an atheistic government, who is their real boss?

For those who do not believe what we are saying, let them see for themselves. They can look into this matter and find that the government decides who is ordained. The government decides who a church's pastor is. It dictates the amount of baptisms allowed per month or year. It dictates how many Bibles can be distributed. The government dictates what can be taught or not taught in the churches, and the government dictates where a pastor can preach and not preach. These are all facts that can be proven. They cannot be denied.

The Bible clearly says that we are one body. We are the Body of Christ. How can we be separated? How can the government tell us that churches in Guiyang cannot fellowship with churches in Kashgar? How can the government tell us that Westerners cannot fellowship with believers in Nanyang? How can the government tell us that Chinese citizens cannot attend international services in Kunming without a foreign passport? The Body of Christ is one body. It cannot, should not, be separated.

You mentioned before that the government controls what is taught in the Three Self Churches of China. How do you know this? You are a part of the underground house church movement. Do you have any proof of these teachings?

Yes. Have you ever been to a Three-Self Church?

No. I attempted a few times in Kunming, some years ago, but because I was a foreigner I was denied entry every time.

Inside the official government churches there are red banners stretched from one side of the room to the other. They are some of the most prominent displays in the churches and are put up by the *Ai Guo* or "love country" movement, also known as the patriotic movement, which reminds all believers that country comes before God. Under those banners is a posting of laws. There are 18 sections or parts on these postings. Some postings have fewer sections and some churches have taken them down all together, but they are still very much a part of the government church in China. Among those postings, the patrons are told that they are forbidden to baptize people under the age of 18, they cannot teach about the resurrection of Jesus Christ, and they can't teach about the Second Coming.

Are these banners still posted at the front of the churches today, in 2009?

Oh yes, they are, and I can take pictures of them and send them to you if you want.

INTERVIEW #2

This interview, with a leader from a different home church network, was conducted in order to provide a different point of view and broader perspective to the reader. The interviewee is the head pastor of a network of about one million believers in Anhui Province.

In America and Europe there are many people claiming that there is growing religious freedom in China. Is this true?

I would agree that there is more religious freedom today than before in most areas.

Are there restrictions on Christians in China? If so, what are they?

Yes. There are many freedoms that we still do not have in China. I know that this is hard for the church in the West to understand. We (the house churches in Anhui) do not have, nor are we allowed to have, an outlet to let the world know the things that we face on a daily basis. Some of the basic tenets of our faith such as fellowship, evangelism, and teaching children about Christian values—these are all forbidden in China.

Christian leaders and pastors from America and Europe have been asked to come and see the practice of Christianity in China. They believe that things are different now, and have even been asked to come and speak at many venues (including churches). During these speaking engagements they have not been told what to speak about and what not to speak about. The number of people present at these events has been extraordinary. After they return to their home countries, they tell others about the freedoms in China. What is your response to this?

Oh, this is a common practice of the Chinese Government. Of course foreigners see these things. It is a show that has been arranged by the government. If they believe what they see during this time, then they believe in a lie.

Do you want proof? Tell the Westerners who say these things after a trip to China that they should arrange another trip to China, but this time to tell the government that they do not need their help. They can arrange their own trip and their own speaking engagements, and they kindly decline the involvement of the government. Then we will see how things go. Only those who want the truth will do this. Others, who continue to repeat what the government has told them, willfully believe a lie.

Many well-known leaders in China are trying to unite the house churches with the government, in an arrangement similar to the Three-Self Church. How do you feel about this?

With the work that we do, it is not possible for me to register.

Why?

One of the greatest problems with this type of an arrangement is that the head of any government church in China would be under the control of an atheist leader. Someone who does not believe in what the Word of God says would be telling us how to practice it. Maybe this is an issue in which others can compromise, but I believe that the Word of God is clear: I must preach the Word, I must reach the lost, I must pray for the sick—these are the things that I must do.

Even if I were to register—where would I register? Any city where I register would be on my license and I would not be able to conduct the work that I do today. I would be unable to travel to other areas and evangelize as I do today all over China. I have been called to preach the Word in many areas of China, how can I agree to stay in just one city?

Many leaders and experts in the West claim that there are enough Bibles in China. What is your response to them?

There are not enough Bibles in China.

Why is that? Is it because the government makes it hard to obtain them, or is it because believers who need Bibles are too poor to purchase their own?

Both. Right now, almost all of our work is in the villages. The people who live in these areas cannot afford Bibles, but this is not the only reason. We are also not able to get access to the number of Bibles that we need.

Many people in the West quote from press releases by Amity Press that there are more than enough Bibles made in China. Do you know that more Bibles are made in China than anywhere else in the world?

When I go to the Three-Self church in Hefei to purchase Bibles, I can buy maybe 5 or 10 without any problem. However, if I purchase large numbers of Bibles or put in a request for numbers exceeding a thousand or so, I am asked why I need so many, where they are going, who they are going to, etc. My information is recorded and maintained by the church authorities as one who has made large purchases. This is not safe for me, so I get my Bibles from an underground press. But did you know that, even with the ability today of registered members to purchase Bibles, there are still not enough for even them. Not even through the official channels.

Are you saying that there are not even enough Bibles available through the Three-Self Church for its own members?

Yes, I am saying that there are not enough Bibles through the official churches. There have been many times when I went to the Hefei Three-Self church to buy only between 5 and 10 Bibles and was turned away because they didn't have any. When strategic meetings take place, at which they determine how to distribute Bibles from the printing office to the Three Self Churches, many negotiations take place. For instance, one church leader might say, "We need one million Bibles." The response from the government official in return might be, "Why do you need so many? You don't need that many. You will only get 200,000." And that is that. End of story.

If you think that there are enough Bibles being printed in China, I urge you to go to the Amity Press website and see how many Bibles they print. Find out how many they send abroad, how many remain in China, and then calculate the number of Three Self churches and the number that they need. After you have done that, figure in that the House Church is much larger than the Three Self Church. Then you will begin to understand the desperate need for Bibles in China.

CONCLUSION

So what is the difference between the underground house churches and the official Three-Self Patriotic Church in China?

In a simple sentence, one is registered and the other is not, but the real situation is more complicated than that. The TSPM is not a denomination. It is unified under the government and officially teaches the basic five tenets of the Christian faith: the Trinity, the deity and humanity of Christ, the Virgin Birth, Christ's Death and Resurrection, and the Second Coming.

The Three Self Patriotic Movement is based on the idea of self-governance, self-support, and self-propagation. These ideas were adopted directly from the Church Missionary Society of the 1800's and were drafted formally in 1892 in Shanghai. The newly formed Communist government officially created this movement in 1954.

During the Cultural Revolution, religious expression in all forms was banned, and it was during this time that all churches were forced underground and the TSPM became virtually extinct. The believers were not allowed to practice their faith openly and went into survival mode. Then, in the early 1980's, the TSPM was reintroduced as a way for the government to infiltrate, subvert, and control organized Christianity.

Because of the way the TSPM churches were founded, there has always been a deep distrust between the underground house churches and the official church. Of course, because China is so large, things can vary from place to place. It should be noted, for example, that there are official churches in Wenzhou that have found common ground with their underground counterparts.

Many people may ask why the underground house churches have to hide the fact that they are Christian. Isn't this against Biblical teachings?

The term "underground" refers to illegal activity and has nothing to do with hiding faith. In fact, the majority of the growth of Christianity in China is due to the "underground" church, not the TSPM. Today most believers, Bible distribution, evangelist activity, and overseas missionary activity are in fact taking place through the underground house churches.

There are TSPM churches that are experiencing revivals and are doing amazing things in the Kingdom of God as well, but the *Back to Jerusalem* vision has always been illegal and, for the most part, is being carried out by the underground house churches.

The house churches are considered to be "underground" because they are illegal; however, they are aggressively evangelizing and reaching the lost. The church in China is growing by tens of thousands of believers every day, in a country where evangelism is illegal, a feat that has not been accomplished in many countries where Christianity is perfectly legal, accepted, and even promoted.

Brother Yun has spent his entire life supporting the vision of *Back to Jerusalem*. He works with Christians in China and around the world for the sake of casting this vision. He works primarily with the underground churches in China because they have committed themselves to carrying out the Great Commission as Christ commanded it, to the ends of the earth.

ACKNOWLEDGEMENTS

We would like to thank Professor Zhou for spending countless hours interviewing Brother Yun in order to write down his story for the first time. We would also like to thank the daughter of missionary parents who transformed the writings of Professor Zhou and put them into digital format as well as editing the 2nd edition of this book. We would also like to thank Haavald Slaaten for first writing the book "The Heavenly Man" and offering his assistance in writing this book. Thanks to MOGEE photography for the pictures included in this work.

Many thanks also to Mr. Shi Tou for the cover design of this book.

We sincerely thank Paul Hattaway for sharing Brother Yun's story with the entire world in a powerful way and for releasing more research and writings on the Chinese church than probably anyone in history. He is truly a living hero of faith and loved by the House church in China.

We would also like to thank Isaac Liu for writing his own personal story about what he remembers from the life of his father in China for the purposes of this book.

CPSIA information can be obtained at www.ICGtesting.com
Printed in the USA
LVOW071652281012
304771LV00018B/145/P